Fundamentalism in Comparative Perspective

Fundamentalism in Comparative Perspective

EDITED BY

Lawrence Kaplan

The University of Massachusetts Press

AMHERST

Copyright © 1992 by
The University of Massachusetts Press
All rights reserved
Printed in the United States of America
LC 91-40973
ISBN 0-87023-797-7 (cloth); 798-5 (pbk.)
Set in Trump Medieval by Keystone Typesetting, Inc.
Printed and bound by Thomson-Shore, Inc.

Library of Congress Cataloging-in-Publication Data
Fundamentalism in comparative perspective / edited by Lawrence Kaplan.
    p. cm.
  Collection of essays presented at the City College of the City
University of New York on May 5, 1988.
  Includes index.
  ISBN 0-87023-797-7 (hard :alk. paper). — ISBN 0-87023-798-5 (pbk.
: alk. paper)
   1. Fundamentalism—Comparative studies—Congresses. I. Kaplan,
Lawrence, 1934–
BL238.F82 1992
291'.09'04—dc20   91–40973
                                               CIP

British Library Cataloguing in Publication data are available.

Chapter 3 first appeared in Steve Bruce, *The Rise and Fall of the New
Christian Right*, © 1988 by Steve Bruce. It is reprinted here, in a slightly
altered form, by permission of Oxford University Press and the author.
Chapter 9 is reprinted from *Religious Radicalism and Politics in the
Middle East*, edited by Emmanuel Sivan and Menachem Friedman by
permission of the State University of New York Press. Copyright © 1990.

Contents

Preface

The subject of fundamentalism, which garnered interest during the 1980s, is as relevant today as ever before. Examples of religious fanaticism, usually accompanied by violence, continue throughout the world with unceasing regularity. Whether the struggles occur among Sikhs, Muslims, and Hindus in India, or between Jew and Muslim in Jerusalem, there are enough instances to remind the informed public that fundamentalism and its ramifications are an ongoing phenomenon. Now with the growing U.S. presence in the Middle East, the interplay of religion and politics in the area must be a consideration for all geopolitical strategies. It is for this reason alone that we believe another work on the subject is warranted.

Considering the importance of fundamentalist religions in our contemporary world, it is surprising that so few recent works comparatively treat fundamentalism's different manifestations. Those that do are Bruce Lawrence's *Defenders of God* (1989), and three collective volumes: Richard T. Antoun and Mary Elaine Hegland, eds., *Religious Resurgence* (1987), Lionel Caplan, ed., *Studies in Religious Fundamentalism* (1987), and Norman J. Cohen, ed., *The Fundamentalist Phenomenon* (1990). Professor Lawrence's work demonstrates how fundamentalism, while very much a product of the modern world, paradoxically decries everything modernism represents. The three collaborative volumes emphasize other aspects of fundamentalism: the Caplan book is heavily weighed toward anthropology; Antoun and Hegland focus on religion as both a cause and an effect of change in modern societies; and Cohen's deals with liberalism's response to the persistent presence of aggressively traditional religions. Yet these few volumes, however excellent, cannot possibly exhaust what is a vast and diversified field. This subject, still in its infancy, can only benefit from extended scholarly coverage.

Similar to the collaborative books cited above, this present work began as a conference. In our case, all but one of the original participants were historians. Three essays (by Bruce, Friedman, and Moghadam) have been added to provide more depth and sociological balance. And this volume includes a lengthy article on the effect of Islamic fundamentalism on women, an area somewhat neglected in other collections. As discussed in the introduction that follows, the antifeminist attitude of most fundamentalists is central to their anger at modernist patterns, and therefore should receive more attention than is generally given in comparative treatments.

The conference that formed the basis of this collection took place at the City College of the City University of New York on May 5, 1988. Several other such conferences were held that year and subsequently. We would like to believe that ours was one of the most successful. The original nature of the contributions encouraged us to publish the proceedings so that a larger audience could benefit. The authors edited their individual contributions, adding the scholarly apparatus they believed necessary to enhance their individual selections.

Any edited volume is, by definition, a joint venture. Above all, appreciation is extended to Milton Glicksman, whose generosity made the entire enterprise possible. The editor would also like to thank Dean Paul Sherwin for his imaginative help in carrying out this endeavor. Valuable suggestions came from two colleagues, Beth Baron and Conrad Schirokauer. And finally, my wife, Carol P. Kaplan, assisted me through the entire process of conference organizing and book producing.

This book is dedicated to the memory of my brother, Leonard B. Kaplan (1933–1987).

December 1990

Fundamentalism in Comparative Perspective

Introduction

We live in an unpredictable time. Few historical guidelines exist to help us assess the developments taking place. One aspect of this new reality has been the sudden and largely peaceful collapse of Eastern European regimes, whose impregnability conventional wisdom had led us to believe was a fact of life. In addition, we have witnessed an undeniable upsurge of powerful irrational forces long thought to be obsolete. Strong nationalistic, even chauvinistic, movements have been erupting in a decade full of startling events. As a result, comfortable intellectual assumptions, which had placed countries and political systems into familiar categories, are constantly being challenged.

In some ways the 1980s commenced in 1979. The Iranian Revolution of that year not only took U.S. leaders by surprise, resulting in a major foreign policy setback, but also served to perplex much of the Western world's educated population. Emerging in a modernizing country allied to the United States was an uncompromising and aggressively anti-American element that threatened to overturn the balance of power in a strategic region. Moreover, the very idea of establishing in the late twentieth century a religious-oriented government whose inspiration allegedly derives from the Middle Ages, proved extremely difficult to assimilate for those bred on conventional assumptions. Two years later, the assassination of Egypt's

Anwar Sadat by fanatic Sunni Muslims, as punishment for his regime's religious shortcomings, reinforced the impression that Iran was not an isolated phenomenon, that fundamentalism was an idea to be reckoned with, and that it possessed world historical significance. The subsequent pronouncement by Middle Eastern leaders of a death sentence on a novelist residing in England, along with threats made to publishers and the firebombing of bookstores elsewhere, reminds us that religious fanaticism continues to affect us all.

It was also in 1979 that the United States witnessed a forceful reassertion of a home-grown variety of fundamentalism—the formation of a new political organization dubbed the "Moral Majority." Fundamentalism had been of some political consequence in the 1920s, yet its impact on American life was believed to have disappeared along with other relics sometime between the New Deal and World War II. Admittedly, with its civic religiosity and relatively large proportion of churchgoers, religion has always played a powerful role in U.S. affairs, while fundamentalism had usually been consigned to a few rural localities where it exerted limited influence on national affairs. But in the 1980s, coinciding with the election of a conservative president, fundamentalism announced itself as an important influence on the national political scene.

Although not always appreciated as such, a return to fundamental principles is often an appealing solution for persons or groups confronting the uncertainties arising from new and seemingly threatening situations. Thus, Protestant reformers in the sixteenth century returned to biblical "certainties" to control the forces unleashed by the Italian Renaissance. But fundamentalism can also take on a secular dimension, as when youthful Chinese Red Guards brandished copies of Mao's *Red Book* during the Cultural Revolution. In this country, conservative intellectuals are alarmed at the changes in university curriculums, and choose to ignore the rich diversity implicit in a world culture. They wish to restrict learning to what they regard as the essential verities of life contained in select Western texts. For these "fundamentalists," the only valid criterion for a proper education in the twentieth century is derived exclusively from a traditional Eurocentric context.

Although the term "fundamentalism" arose from a uniquely

American situation among Protestants early in this century, it has been applied to religious movements as diverse as Twelve Imam Shi'ites, Sikhs, and Sinhalese on the Indian subcontinent, Pentecostals in South America, and Israeli settlers on the West Bank, as well as to smaller sects throughout the world. Obviously the term is imprecise and an oversimplification, but somehow it has managed to take hold. Professor Marty, in the first essay of this collection, cogently explains the legitimacy of its usage (see Chapter 1). Almost exclusively applied to religious groups, fundamentalism will be defined anew by practically every one of this book's authors. For the purposes of this introduction, fundamentalism can be described as a world view that highlights specific essential "truths" of traditional faiths and applies them with earnestness and fervor to twentieth-century realities. This particular mindset is only of consequence, and therefore worthy of attention, when it becomes politically potent, altering what had been considered the normal and predictable parameters of a country's political life.

There is no question that fundamentalism as a contemporary phenomenon has almost as many different origins as it has varying national manifestations, it also has certain uniform themes. In the United States, fundamentalism's earliest progenitors some seventy years ago directed their attention to liberal developments within established Protestant churches. They set down uncompromising fundamentals, mainly connected with biblical inerrancy, that defined what they considered the basis of "true Christianity." Clifford Geertz, in his *Islam Observed* (1968), suggests the use of the term "Scripturalism" to describe the rise of a radical, uncompromising purism that sought to reestablish in both Indonesia and Morocco its version of the original Islam of the Prophet. More recently, as Professor Coleman observes, the Integralism movement shares this same kind of desire to rid the Catholic church of its "false" values and teachings (see Chapter 4). Thus, in one of its primary manifestations, fundamentalism arises as a reaction against either the introduction of modern concepts into traditional religions or, more commonly, against the adjustments of doctrine that are often carried out by reformist elements who wish to make long-standing precepts more suitable to contemporary tastes.

The revolt of these militant preservers of orthodoxy and tradition points out fundamentalism's principal characteristic: its seeming rejection of modernization—"seeming," because certain fundamentalist groups are only too willing to use, and in many instances are quite expert at using, the most advanced technologies of the modern era. This is particularly evident in the United States, where televangelists skillfully manipulate the mass media to great advantage. And Moral Majority lobbyists, demonstrate their state-of-the-art lobbying skills by effectively using computer listings and direct mailings. In Israel, representatives of the Ultra-Orthodox reject modernity, yet appear on the country's only TV network to promote their views. In Iran, followers of the Ayatollah Khomeini shrewdly used tape recorders and cassettes to undermine the shah, and continue to employ sophisticated progandistic techniques to solidify their hold on the modern state apparatus. Nevertheless, there is little question that the faithful regard modernity, along with its values based on secularist Enlightenment thought, as the chief threat to varying forms of fundamentalism the world over.

Universally, an inevitable tension exists between the scientific nature of modernization and all orthodox religions. While most religions are able to adjust, some observers—and Bassam Tibi (1988) goes the furthest here—assert that Islam is by definition incompatible with the technological-scientific culture of the modern world. By rejecting the principles of tolerance, rationality, and secularity, a major strand of Islam condemns itself to remaining a preindustrial culture, thereby defending against the introduction of foreign elements (i.e., modernity). Since modernity can never satisfy the human search for spirituality, the Egyptian Sunni theorist Sayyid Qutb argued that modernity would have to be vigorously opposed. Similar sentiments have often been expressed by Shi'ite leaders.

A theme reiterated by Third World Islamic fundamentalists is the "failure of the West," by which they mean that the Euro-American emphasis on materialism, luxury, and consumerism has led to the destruction of human values and resulted in moral decay, including the breakdown of family structures and the spread of pornography. This is why Khomeini, in his famous 1989 letter to Gorbachev, warned about exchanging materialistic Marxism for the equally, or perhaps worse, species of materialism associated with the Western way of life. "I strongly urge you," he wrote shortly before his death, "that in breaking down the walls of Marxist fantasies you do not fall into the prison of the West and the Great Satan" (quoted in Esposito, 1990).

To be sure, this vigorous rejection of a heartless "Westoxication" was a key ideological element of the Shi'ite revolution in Iran. Some of these themes, including an attack on individualistic materialism, can be found among the Gush Emunim faithful in Israel. This is an interesting sharing of views by extremist Jews and Muslims, and not the only instance where radical branches of these two Middle Eastern religions coincide. Curiously, U.S. fundamentalists stand alone in this regard by virtue of their eager acceptance of the "American way of life," which includes many of the individualistic values decried by their counterparts elsewhere (e.g., consumerism, good living, and individualism).

Although a modern industrialized society would seem to be a highly desirable long-range goal, it does not inevitably improve the living standards of a country's population. From the days of England's "satanic mills," there has always been a price to pay in human suffering during the transition from an agrarian society to an industrial and urban one. But in this century, especially in the Third World, economic progress often breeds rural impoverishment and urban blight on a dimension not previously experienced in the West. Moreover, the ills befalling these newly urbanizing societies—among them slums, homelessness, malnutrition, and crime—continue indefinitely, indeed seem to be permanent results of the modernization process.

The societal dislocation that inevitably accompanies industrialization and urban growth has long been a source of social discontent. Going back at least to Durkheim, in the late nineteenth century, social theorists have long recognized that the breakdown of rural community life leaves rootless people with problems of identity, nostalgic for past associations, and susceptible to simplistic alternatives to anomie. In the 1930s the consequences of rootlessness often manifested themselves in nativistic and totalitarian movements. Recent comparative treatments of the Iranian Revolution—

and Abrahamian's essay in this volume is one of the most original—
have found similarities between the generalized Shi'ite message and
twentieth-century fascism as well as an authoritarian form of populism (see Chapter 6; and also Cole and Keddie, 1986). Accordingly,
scholars have observed that in many Middle Eastern countries new
arrivals to the cities become the most fervent adherents of the fundamentalist message.

One by-product of urbanization which a traditional rural population finds difficult to accept is the changing role played by women.
Herein lies an important explanation for orthodox religions' opposition to an essential ingredient of the modernization process: they
fervently resent all attempts made to liberate women. For if it is true
that an important index for the progress of humanity is measured by
the equality of the sexes—as nineteenth-century socialists like Fou-
rier, Saint Simon, and Engels suggested—then fundamentalist religions are distinctly premodern. Indeed, with very few exceptions,
fundamentalists react with great negative emotion to women's liberation, and their unmistakable hysteria must be seen as central to the
"true believer's" fanaticism. Unfortunately, it is an aspect that rarely
gets the attention it deserves.

In the United States, the Moral Majority and their cohorts oppose
the Equal Rights Amendment and the option of a woman's choice to
terminate pregnancy. But this level of interference with the rights of
women pales when compared to the restrictions placed on women in
traditionalist Muslim countries. The repressiveness becomes even
more severe when fundamentalists are in power, as in Saudi Arabia,
in Afghan refugee camps in Pakistan, and in the regime of the ayatollahs. For the Scripturalist, Muslim women are insatiable beings who
must be controlled in behavior and dress; according to this mindset,
an unveiled woman is essentially naked. Thus, if women are not
closely monitored and carefully supervised, they will lead males
down Satan's road of perdition, first undermining the family, which
in turn will destroy the very foundations of the Muslim community.

The extent of Ayatollah Khomeini's hostility toward women has
not been given adequate attention in general treatments of fundamentalism. This traditional point of view goes way beyond the call to
restore the veil, and is among the most retrograde found in main-

stream Islamic thought. Some of his ideas border on the bizarre. That women, in his teaching, are to be totally subservient to their husband's will needs hardly be stressed. But he goes further: men should not accept their wives' claims to be menstruating or entering menopause as justifications for avoiding sex. Rather, husbands should be guided by some arbitrary calculations that the ayatollah himself has contrived in order to overcome the wiles of their women. There are other strange opinions offered on such intimate concerns as vaginal discharges and the suitability of oral sex. In civil matters women are to be discriminated against in various ways. For instance, two female witnesses are the equivalent of one male. With the reintroduction of the medieval concept of "blood justice," the killing of a man is considered a capital crime, but a woman's murder is not of the same dimension and would rarely result in equivalent penalties (Afshar, 1982). Another example of radical Islam's bias against women can be found in Afghanistan and Dr. Valentine Moghadam makes a strong case for the centrality of this issue (see Chapter 7).

A troubling corollary of fundamentalism's general negativity toward modern women is the fact that the movement seems to be most popular among lower-class women, who for various reasons feel threatened by the options and flexibility modern society has to offer. The strongest adherents in the United States are elderly rural women, while in the Middle East first-generation urban females provide the largest single group consistently devoted to Islamic fundamentalism. One of the greatest ironies connected with the overthrow of the shah was that even middle-class, liberated women served the revolution in various capacities, especially in large demonstrations, and in this regard helped to bring about their own downfall. But they were not the only progressive forces in Iran who failed to predict the viciousness of a radical Islamic regime supported by the instruments of modern control (another irony), and consequently to suffer in the aftermath; for as mentioned above, there were no recent historical precedents to guide them.

A further explanation for the overwhelming support given by liberated women and other secularists to a revolution led by militant Muslims was its populist orientation, whose generalized appeal focused on the oppressiveness of a shah allied to Western imperialism.

All previous forms of protest against the government having been eliminated, radical Islam proved to have remarkable staying power, not easily eradicated even by Savak's modern techniques of repression. In the end it became a most effective mobilizing ideology. The statements of its spokesmen were vague and diffuse enough to appeal to different classes in Iranian society, permitting the country's disaffected elements to unite behind the clerical faction, which ultimately became the only group capable of rallying the masses.

In this connection, Professor Sivan's essay (see Chapter 5) demonstrates how religion in Iran preserved a key aspect of civil society against the onslaughts of the shah's modernizing hegemony, thereby providing the basis for eventual rebellion. Sivan's sophisticated use of a Gramscian thesis is extremely suggestive, for it offers possible explanations as to how certain oppositional ideologies can survive in authoritarian societies. This is particularly true of traditional religions, with which a generally repressive state might be reluctant to tamper: an example of this phenomenon is the continued existence of Roman Catholicism in Communist Poland as a viable unassimilative institution. And the survival of a fractious, long-smoldering nationalism which has reemerged vigorously in present-day Eastern Europe can also be appreciated within Sivan's formulation.

Another reason that fundamentalist religions persist in authoritarian state settings is that the "true believer's" penchant for martyrdom provides constant evidence of unshakable dedication. Considering the temptations for co-option and compromise within the dominant modern culture, outward manifestations of idealism combined with the sufferings of a number of martyrs prove to be extremely compelling, winning support for the movement. In almost every country studied, the "armed prophets" of religion, like those Arthur Hertzberg describes in Israel, gain the respect of elements in the general population who are not necessarily committed to their scriptural interpretations (see Chapter 8). To be sure, only in the materialistic American culture can TV evangelists openly display their enormous wealth and yet present themselves as dedicated servants of God.

One tendency shared by fundamentalists who impact on politics is their ability to move the political agenda further to the right, indicating their invariably conservative, if not reactionary, influence. Fundamentalists, by definition, are anti-Communists, and anti-Socialists as well. With Communism on the decline throughout most of the world, Catholic Integralists now regard Liberation Theology as an equally dangerous doctrine to be forcefully opposed. In Israel, both the Gush Emunim faithful, with their special brand of innovative fundamentalism, and the traditionalist Neturei Karta, have had a distinct conservative impact on their country's politics (see Menachem Friedman's article, Chapter 9). The appellation most frequently used for fundamentalists in the United States is "the new Christian right." Steve Bruce demonstrates in his book (1988) how the formation of the Moral Majority was a conscious design of right-wing secular Republicans to further their political goals. For in this country the successful promotion of noneconomic values as political issues has enabled conservatives to win electoral victories from a population whose awareness of its own self-interests is underdeveloped. In many ways, the flourishing existence of a new Christian right in the United States best exemplifies fundamentalism as political manipulation.

It can be argued similarly that Islamic fundamentalism, especially in its Shi'ite version, permits a traditionally minded clergy to manipulate the masses for its own advantage. Because the Islamic clerics and scholars are the only "experts" in the content of the sacred texts, they have become a privileged elite, ready to carry out in practice "the exact meaning" of said texts. It follows, therefore, that the monopoly of state power can be entrusted only to these men, who become the religious equivalents of Lenin's vanguard party. The results of their successes, from a political perspective, are equally undemocratic. If we choose here to paraphase Marx when he said that history occurs first as tragedy and then as farce, we would not do justice to the sorrowful manifestations of revolutionary terrorism in its Islamic configuration.

As a generation disillusioned by the experiences of command societies, we can quickly recognize that those who stand to gain from a return to "fundamentals" are those who present themselves as the sole authorities on scriptural interpretation. Ironically, nowhere do these sacred texts (i.e., the Koran) discuss such a role for the clergy. In fact, an established clergy is not mentioned in the Koran at all, nor for that matter is there any reference in the Muslim corpus or tradition to an Islamic *republic,* a most modern conception invented by Khomeini (Roy, 1986).

It is not difficult to point out contradictions in the statements of various fundamentalist groups as they attempt to impose traditional religions on twentieth-century realities. Some of the most obvious are to be found among those in the United States who are convinced that sin (e.g., homosexuality, abortion, pornography, lack of prayer in schools, the teaching of evolution, etc.) is rapidly overtaking our land, yet who still assert that ours is God's country and that "Americanism" is synonymous with godliness. Religion, herein, is used as a prop for a nationalistic defense of the existing social order, despite a growing awareness of this country's moral imperfections. Another example of inconsistency is when fundamentalists join political conservatives to oppose encroachments of state power, and at the same time call for government involvement in the most intimate matters in order to enforce their version of acceptable personal behavior (Barr, 1977).

While U.S. fundamentalists have not markedly changed moral patterns in this country, the Shi'ites, from their position of power in Iran, have succeeded in mandating a puritanical code of behavior with cruel efficiency. In other Islamic societies Muslim fundamentalists have managed to reverse a secularization of social customs; one can see, for example, the return of the veil among university women in Egypt and even in such a secular nation as Turkey. Moreover, in almost every Muslim country in the Middle East as well as in Asia, political leaders must remain conscious of the fundamentalist presence so as not to offend sensibilities. Thus, radical Islam remains an important fact of life in many parts of the world. Reports of moderating tendencies in Iran have proved to be wishful thinking. The ayatollahs have survived a catastrophic war with Iraq as well as a precipitous decline in living standards, and all evidence points to the probability that they will endure for the foreseeable future. With their failure to export their version of the Islamic revolution, we might very well see history repeating itself, in that full Islamization has been limited (as was the case with socialism and Russia) to one country.

In the United States, because of the discrediting of certain well-known evangelists and the disappearance of the Moral Majority, it would be easy to write off the new Christian right as a failure. Indeed, many social scientists have already produced analyses to explain its diminished visibility (Steve Bruce puts forth this argument quite persuasively in Chapter 3). Nevertheless, Professor Ribuffo is perhaps correct to advise caution in this regard, in that earlier epitaphs have proven to be premature. Thus, one should be somewhat tentative in confidently predicting future events (see Chapter 2).

The declining economic position of the United States in the world, for example, might provide a favorable environment for the resurrection of a new version of dispensationalism, or an even more extreme form of apocalyptic Protestantism. Moreover, as the United States further involves itself in Middle Eastern affairs, with the distinct possibility of installing a permanent presence in the region, anti-Western tendencies of a religious character might erupt in a way that frustrates geopolitical strategies. Secular regimes or movements in this highly volatile area of the world, which are seen to compromise with "the Great Satan" or its allies, could very well jeopardize their mandate.

As we suggested at the outset of this introduction, unexpected developments now characterize contemporary world affairs, a fact that should encourage restraint rather than overextension at the present juncture of events. We should be less confident than some of our Enlightenment forebears that rational modernity will inevitably overcome the remnants of irrational traditionalism. Fundamentalism, because of its easily comprehended appeal, remains one of the alternatives that people in various cultures seize when encountering the diverse traumas of modernity. All we can say with assurance is that as long as human suffering and uncertainty persist, fundamentalism will continue to be one of the options utilized to explain the world and to promise solace. There are good reasons to believe that it will remain an important part of our experience well into the twenty-first century.

Bibliography

Afshar, Haleh. "Khomeini's Teachings and Their Implications for Iranian Women." In *The Women's Movement in Iran*, ed. Azar Tabari and Nahid Yeganeh. London, 1982.

———. *Iran, A Revolution in Turmoil*. Albany, N.Y., 1985.

Antoun, Richard T., and Mary Elaine Hegland, eds. *Religious Resurgence*. Syracuse, N.Y., 1987.

Arojomand, Said Amir. *The Turban for the Crown*. New York, 1988.

Avineri, Shlomo. *The Making of Modern Zionism*. New York, 1981.

Bakhash, Shaul. *The Reign of the Ayatollahs*. New York, 1984.

Barr, James. *Fundamentalism*. Philadelphia, 1977/78.

Berger, Peter. *Facing Up to Modernity*. New York, 1977.

Bruce, Steve. *The Rise and Fall of the New Christian Right*. Oxford, 1988.

Caplan, Lionel, ed. *Studies in Religious Fundamentalism*. Albany, N.Y., 1987.

Cohen, Norman, ed. *The Fundamentalist Phenomenon*. Grand Rapids, Mich., 1990.

Cole, Juan, and Nikki Keddie, eds. *Shiism and Social Protest*. New Haven, 1986.

Esposito, John L., ed. *The Iranian Revolution, Its Global Impact*. Miami, 1990.

Geertz, Clifford. *Islam Observed*. New Haven, 1968.

Hiro, Dilip. *Holy Wars: The Rise of Islamic Fundamentalism*. New York, 1989.

Kepel, Gilles. *Muslim Extremism in Egypt*. Berkeley, 1984.

Lawrence, Bruce B. *Defenders of God*. San Francisco, 1989.

Liebman, Robert C., and Robert Wuthnow, eds. *The New Christian Right*. New York, 1983.

Marsden, George M. *Fundamentalism and American Culture*. New York, 1980.

Roy, Oliver. *Islam and Resistance in Afghanistan*. Cambridge, England, 1986.

Sivan, Emmanuel. *Radical Islam: Medieval Theology and Modern Politics*. New Haven, 1985.

Sivan, Emmanuel, and Menachem Friedman, eds. *Religious Radicalism and Politics in the Middle East*. Albany, N.Y., 1990.

Tibi, Bassam. *The Crisis of Modern Islam*. Salt Lake City, 1988.

Wright, Robin. *In the Name of God*. New York, 1989.

Wuthnow, Robert. *The Restructuring of American Religion*. Princeton, 1988.

1

Fundamentals of Fundamentalism

Martin E. Marty

To speak of "the" fundamentals of fundamentalism would signal arrogance. Yet any effort to describe international fundamentalisms, as we are doing in this volume, demands at least some sort of hypothesis. We need heuristic devices to begin a search. "Fundamentals," then, refers to some distinctive, not necessarily unique, features of movements called fundamentalist. They need not be present in the same way or same measure in all such movements, but they should be characteristic of most of them.

A word, first, about the spirit of the inquiry. Spinoza set forth some terms. In his tract on politics the philosopher said that when he set out to study human actions, he made a sedulous effort not to laugh, not to cry, not to denounce, but to understand. It is easy to have emotions roused on this controversial topic, and this author brings preconceptions. But the main goal is to hold such attitudes sufficiently in suspension that we can begin to understand.

We begin in the spirit of Edmund Husserl's imaged explorer. This explorer comes across what is to him a trackless place. If it has been mapped, he does not know this. He can discern certain outlines: a hill, high trees, or whatever, but he must make his way through it, noting and charting as he goes. So we come across the islands called fundamentalisms, and begin noting, charting, and then naming.

This approach begins with a kind of naive nominalism. Given: that every day in the newspapers one reads or on radio and television one hears about movements that in English language transmission are called "fundamentalism." Of course, it cannot mean exactly the same thing everywhere. Yet the term enters the vocabulary to designate a class of things that have some common features. In a certain period, "Left" and "Right" come into use. No one pretends that the Left and the Right in French politics means the same thing as in American religion, yet the terms point to phenomena which demand and deserve some common inquiry. Alexis de Tocqueville invents "individualism;" someone else invents "technology;" a third comes up with "bureaucracy." Of course, each has long historical antecedents and many varieties. Yet the terms have uses, and it would be futile to try to suppress them in each case. So it is with the invention of "fundamentalism" and its analogies elsewhere. The nominalist says: Here I come across a term, a usage; to what does it point?

For the record, the word began to be used in the United States in July 1920, during a dispute within conservative Protestantism. A party of contenders chose that name for itself, and the heirs still wear the badge proudly.

Why bother with it? Why not study each phenomenon in utter isolation, complete singularity? Answer: because historical, sociological, and philosophical inquiries are often informed by comparative approaches. Philosopher Morris Cohen liked to remind that the absolutely unique, that which has no element in common with anything else, is indescribable, since all description and all analysis are in terms of predicates, class concepts, or repeatable relations. And the great French historian Marc Bloch wrote that comparativism comes up whenever one is involved with efforts at explanation. One needs some question, some hypothesis, and then the comparative approach necessarily comes up. So it is with movements around the world today.

The comparative approach can serve not only intellectual but also "public policy" needs. Thus, epidemiologists study the AIDS outbreak in Africa and America in order to determine distinctive features that may call forth differing diagnoses and treatments. In the comparative approach one sees common features but then can note differences in the two locales in respect to heterosexual versus homosexual cohort outbreaks, and the like. Or actuaries might study long-lived people in Azerbaijan and in Utah to see whether folk life in the two places can explain why people tend to live longer there than in many other places. Utah's residents are Mormon, and their way of life has something to do with longevity. The Azerbaijanis are not. Can a comparative approach help determine what the two populations might have in common?

Whoever compares has to keep singularity in mind. One is reminded of William James's empathy for the crab who does not want simply to be classified and dismissed as a crustacean. No, I am a crab; I am "me." So it is for people who come to be called (in this case in English and increasingly in translations) fundamentalist. Scholars who are well versed in the separate cultures often speak up for these singularities and try to establish and patent alternative words. I have read of some who say that the subculture they study might more accurately be called, say, "belligerent neoradical protorevolutionary extremist conservatism," or whatever. They have already lost their battle to establish such a term, and ordinarily when they describe the phenomenon in question, it shares many features with movements called, elsewhere, fundamentalism. It is possible to keep "me, the crab" in mind while also studying crustaceans. Every comparativist knows to do that.

Let me make two other preliminary qualifying statements. For the first, one is tempted to use capital letters to emphasize a point. SUBSTANTIVELY, FUNDAMENTALISMS HAVE LITTLE OR NOTHING IN COMMON WITH EACH OTHER. The whole point of, say, Shi'ite Islamic fundamentalism is to locate, insist on, and apply fundamental elements of *shari'a*,—law codes—which Islam shares with none of the other faiths or world views from which it would distance itself. Again, when Protestants reach for fundamentals, they reach precisely for unsharable teachings, for features that are distinctive to Christian faith claims, e.g., about a literal second coming of Jesus.

Next to that let us bracket the effort to determine what role individual psychology plays in fundamentalisms. Such a study has much to tell, but it is not the present point. I simply am resisting psychological reductionisms here, efforts to say that this or that individual turns fundamentalist because, say, she was toilet trained too early, or he is oedipal, or they suffered teen traumas. Such efforts do not easily explain why a whole population on one side of a mountain, a river, a map line, is fundamentalist and another cohort or population on another side remains simply conservative.

Now, to some "fundamentals of fundamentalism."

1. Fundamentalisms occur on the soil of *traditional* cultures, or cultures in which people perceive and claim that they simply and conservatively inherit a world view and way of life. From Al-Ghazzali to the present, one comes to know that most people who live in traditional cultures do not know they are traditionalist. They do not see the "other," and are untested. Thus newly established intense religious groups (sometimes still called "cults," especially pejoratively) are not fundamentalist, even if socially they bear some marks of fundamentalist movements. There has to be a previously unassaulted, relatively protected traditionalist culture, within which a body of people has some sense that there was a true or pure ancestral past.

Now, if a movement is only conservative, traditional, orthodox, or classical, I like to observe that "we"—scholars, mass communicators, politicians, publics—would pay little or no attention to them, certainly not as a class. A lonely anthropologist may tape-record a tribe in its singularities, or a sociologist might drive past a Baptist church in some hollow or other. Fundamentalisms occur or get named in different circumstances. I have heard Clifford Geertz cited as having observed and claimed that "from now on no one will leave anyone else alone." I presume he refers to advertising, mass media, travel, mass higher education, attempts at persuasion, propaganda, and proselytism. When traditional cultures no longer feel "left alone" or when they want to intrude on "the other" of whom they become aware, something happens to tradition—that which was conserved, the beliefs or practices that come to be regarded as classical and orthodox.

2. The second element is a widespread if vague sense of threat. Usually the threat is focused. Peter Laslett speaks of "the world we have lost." People tend toward fundamentalism when they fear losing a world. Such threats may come from outside the group, and are

given code words like "Westernization" or "modernity" or "invasion," coupled with "pluralism" or "secularism" or whatever. Or threats may come from within, as when someone in a group turns innovator, experimenter, adapter. What Walter Lippmann called "the acids of modernity" do not always penetrate from without.

Thus when in traditional cultures someone chooses to adapt to modernity, however defined, by becoming "modernist," he or she becomes a challenger. The revisionist who reworks the sacred history of the group assaults it. Radical reformulators are threats. Reinterpretation to meet the challenge of a new day demands counteraction. If there is "symbolization" or "spiritualization" of a heritage, guardians of the tradition smell change; they get their backs up and plan resistance.

3. Most briefly, and already hinted at, in the population there must be some generalized uneasiness, discontent, fear of identity diffusion, or loss of focus. And leaders must emerge who give names to the discontented and who can name the challengers, the enemies; these may be apostates or heretics, or they may be subtle phenomena like "secular humanism."

4. Now comes reaction. So far as those who pursue these hypotheses are concerned, the term "fundamentalism" is first applied when leaders and followers take steps consciously to react, to innovate, to defend, and to find new ways to counter what they perceive as threats to the tradition they would conserve. You might say they become "busy." Reaction, counteraction, revanchist action: these are characteristic. If they are not present, observers continue to call movements or cultures simply "traditional" or "conservative."

5. The counteraction takes the form of discriminating reclamations. There may be some separation, by leaders, between "fundamentals" and "nonfundamentals." That division must be at least hypothetically present; why else point to "fundamentals"? Of course, most fundamentalists might think of the heritage as a "package deal," and may argue that they cannot yield on even a small point lest a larger one be compromised. Yet they are selective about what from the past must be seen and insisted upon as fundamental.

Catholicism is an elaborate and intricate system of belief and behavior patterns and elements. The Catholic fundamentalist may overlook the grand fundamentals such as the Trinity, or this or that Christological view. She will instead select items that will "stand out," such as mass in Latin, opposition to women priests, optional clerical celibacy, or support for papal dismissals of "artificial birth control." These selective retrievals issue in the application of the term "fundamentalist."

So it is also with American Protestants, on whose soil the self-chosen term first prospered. When challenged by "modernity" outside Protestantism and "modernism" (e.g., biblical criticism, evolutionary thought in the seminaries) the party that called itself "fundamentalist" did not reach back to—or, of course, deny—central teachings such as the doctrine of the Trinity of the Chalcedonian formula of Christology. It rarely mentioned the sacraments, over which the movement was itself divided and where it had to allow diversity. It chose a different set of teachings and assigned them "fundamental" status. This move includes at least two characteristic features, our next two fundamental points.

6. Fundamentalists seek authority. This may reside in exaggerated views of hierarchical authority, such as papal infallibility. It may refer to a law book, or a story, or a classic event. Almost always there will be an insistence on an authoritative set of texts, a canon that is an inerrant utterance of the final truth about reality. Without such an assured, specifiable authority as that provided by shari'a or "the inerrant Bible," it would be difficult to hold a movement together, to ward off outsiders, or to have a good argument. While the text is usually regarded as sacred, secular philosophies such as Marxism are able to produce movements of selective retrieval which appeal to authoritative texts as a way to start and sometimes finish arguments.

7. The other common feature of the fundamental insistences, be they doctrinal, practical, behavioral, or cultural, is that they offend, they "cause scandal." The Greek word for offense is *skandalon*, which evokes the idea of tripping or trapping. Fundamentalist teachings or insistences are chosen and designed to "trap" those who would evade them, to "trip" those who would transgress them. They are not chosen in order to commend the movement to the outside world.

Thus, when television cameras close in on Iranians who stone an adulterous couple or sever the hand of the guilty pickpocket after trial, "outsiders" feel revulsion and alienation. They are supposed to. When Protestant fundamentalist denominations fight on camera over the "literal" saga of the prophet Jonah being eaten by a great fish, which spews him up days later, the outsider laughs and scorns, and one would expect public relations' experts within the movement to minimize the scandal of the teaching. Instead, these experts want the larger public exposed to such a teaching.

One might use the image of the castle. One needs thick walls, fastnesses, a "keep" for the people within. One needs towers and battlements from which to try to keep others out, or drawbridges over which the party within can make forays to clear space and keep enemies at a distance. And there must be a moat, into which those who would transgress from either direction would sink.

8. Let us talk about the moat. Fundamentalisms resist ambiguity and ambivalence. You have to be "this" or "that." To borrow from sectarian philosophy or theology, there is a temptation even in cultures that do not know the name to be "Manichaean." This means that the universe is clearly divided under the hegemonies of Good versus Evil. This may sometimes translate to Christ versus Antichrist, in a Christian culture, or God versus Satan. There is a war on, perhaps based on a "war in heaven," as in Milton's *Paradise Lost,* Book VI, based on a biblical clue, with its reflection of war on earth. The enemy is compromise or the compromiser. The potential apostate or heretic is threatened with drowning in the figurative moat.

9. On the basis of this sharp metaphysical-type division, there is then a practical division through the formation of a people. Fundamentalisms often rely on cultural "thickness," on tribalism, on people's blood relations and physical propinquity. Yet they also can rely on what has been called "convergent selectivity," as when people are summoned across distances by mass media of communication. They may wear insignia, or learn shibboleths and code words or behavior patterns which lead them to recognize each other.

In either case, something like "the party of God" or "the people of God" or "the chosen people" or "the elect" emerges—a Moral Majority, if you will, that has found each other and will oppose outsiders, infidels, waverers, adapters.

10. Fundamentalisms then become potentially or actually aggressive. Many newcomers to the scene of reportage equate fundamentalisms with belligerence and militancy, with terrorism or revolution, with shooting and killing, or with massive efforts to take over a polity, as through constitutional amendment in a republic. Yet fundamentalist movements may long satisfy people with private interests, who may wish to be left alone, as if sectarian; they want to be free to bring up their children in their pattern, as nonfundamentalist traditionalists like the Amish or the Doukhobors choose to do.

Yet there must be a potential, if the people are agents of God or of a transcendent philosophy or force, for them to erupt from passivity into activity. Given the stakes, the scale of challenges, and the instruments of change made possible in a technological era, the move toward activism and aggression may be quite rapid. The first movement—the politics of withdrawal—then characteristically changes into a politics of resentment. Fundamentalists resent being left out, deprived, displaced, scorned, marginalized. They feel their cultures penetrated. They must take action against the infidel. There is almost always a polity implication, whether constitutional, revolutionary, or designed to stabilize a hegemony of fundamentalists.

11. Finally, the comparativist looks for and, so far as I know, finds what we might call encompassing, substantive philosophies of history in fundamentalisms. They deal with the future as if it had already occurred, measuring history and their actions from such futures. This means that they are, in many religious traditions, messianic and millennial. They may act in the name of the assured revolution of the proletariat which produces a classless society, or a coming Golden Age or Paradise, or the Second Coming of Jesus. It is possible that the philosophy of history could be progressive, but the more common pattern is for apocalyptic, dramatic upheavals in the course of events.

Such a philosophy of history for the group and the individual permits one to live with setback and postponement. While fundamentalisms are multiclass phenomena—the recent ones in America took off in middle-class cultures, and not just among the poor—often they give solace and meaning to the deprived. The future is assured, the past was grand, the present may be cloudy. Yet the philosophy of history grants to insiders enough knowledge about and motivation from a specific future and discernible past to help members follow prescriptive paths and actions in the present.

When they look thus, believe thus, live thus, and hope thus, observers call them fundamentalist, and most have cognate or analogous terms to describe themselves. They have become major contenders on the world scene late in the twentieth century, in a time when progressives thought they would all have been fossilized or would simply have disappeared. They merit study both comparatively, for what they hold in common, and in their singularity.

2

American Fundamentalism to the 1950s: A Guide for New Yorkers

LEO P. RIBUFFO

Unlike other great cities, New York is not usually associated with fundamentalism. Walking through downtown Chicago, we can easily encounter the Moody Bible Institute, whose founder, Dwight L. Moody, emerged as the nation's foremost evangelist in the 1870s and built a religious infrastructure later used by fundamentalists. Chicago is also home to the Pacific Garden Mission, where Billy Sunday, Moody's successor as the premier American evangelist, returned to Christ in 1886. And Los Angeles houses the Angelus Temple, where the great, gorgeous Pentecostal preacher, Aimee Semple McPherson, held forth from the 1920s until her death in 1944.

The absence of comparable landmarks in New York City reflects the relative weakness of the fundamentalist movement there. Yet, paradoxically, New York has played a decisive role in the *interpretation* of fundamentalism. Indeed, three CCNY alumni—Daniel Bell, '38, Seymour Martin Lipset, '43, and Nathan Glazer, '44—offered an explanation of fundamentalism that survived virtually unchallenged among social scientists from the mid-1950s until the late 1970s. According to Bell, Lipset, and Glazer, fundamentalism was best understood as a social movement led by provincials whose penchant for far-fetched conspiracy theories rose as their status declined. Although this pluralist theory contains several grains of truth, those granules are now usually diluted in popularizations by journalists or polemical mailings from People for the American Way. Moreover, even sophisticated versions—presented, for example, in Bell's famous anthology, *The New American Right* (first published in 1955, then revised and reissued as *The Radical Right* in 1963)—are problematical products of a venerable cultural conflict between cosmopolitan intellectuals and theologically conservative Protestants. In the 1990s, still, neither side understands the other very well.

In this chapter, an attempt to maximize understanding, I will consider aspects of theologically conservative Protestantism from the late nineteenth century until the 1950s, when this broad religious movement underwent an important transition. We will see that New York City, though lacking in fundamentalist landmarks, did house some fundamentalist activists, many targets of fundamentalist ire, and even a few empathic cosmopolitans who tried to make sense of that anger.

Most thoughtful Americans probably know that a hundred years ago our country was overwhelmingly Protestant. What needs emphasis, however, is the degree to which an evangelical Protestant ethos pervaded the cultural elite and, to a lesser but large extent, affected everyday life. Of course all American Protestants were not alike. Their faith had been marked by schism and internecine persecution from the outset; Mormons could attest that neither had ceased by the late nineteenth century. Nonetheless, especially after the Civil War settled the central issue of slavery, there was sufficient agreement among major denominations to make possible an evangelical coalition promoting piety, diligence, temperance, and patriotism, traits often presented as characteristically if not exclusively Protestant. Catholics and Jews represented significant minorities, enjoyed equality before the law, and sometimes rose to positions of power, nonetheless, their faiths definitely were affected by the prevailing ethos. As Professor Glazer has suggested, a merger between Reform Judaism and modernist Protestantism would not have been inconceivable a hundred years ago. And the American Catholic hierarchy, skeptical of papal infallibility and ostentatiously devoted to the Constitution, was more tolerant than most of its European counterparts.

In 1876 leading Protestants would have agreed with Rev. Henry

Ward Beecher of Brooklyn, who declared during a celebration of the nation's centennial that Americans were now richer, wiser, and more devout than ever before. To Beecher and millions of his fellow citizens, the Union victory in the Civil War proved that God had tested but ultimately blessed America. During the next quarter century, even the smuggest American (and Beecher was surely a contender for the title) had reason to wonder about God's purposes, let alone His nationality. Shrewd entrepreneurs created an impressive industrial plant, managed financially potent oligopolies, and attracted cheap labor from the American and European countryside. Yet prosperity trickled down slowly and sometimes collapsed altogether. With good reason—and inflated rhetoric—small farmers and industrial workers blamed the conspicuously consuming elite for unemployment, injury, and impoverishment. After a deep depression began in 1893, American society faced another great test. To many observers the fall of Rome seemed a truer parallel than Christ's entry into Jerusalem.

Extraordinary as these social changes were, they probably created less anguish among leading Protestants than did the intellectual challenges to casually accepted religious beliefs. That only a minority of Protestant clergy ultimately endorsed a social gospel suggests that it was easier to ignore conspicuously consuming sinners than to ignore proponents of Darwinism and biblical higher criticism. The theory of evolution, widely known by the 1880s, implied that mankind was only slightly superior to apes rather than slightly inferior to angels. Although higher criticism—the study of the Bible in texts as close to the original as possible—was not so widely disseminated as Darwinism, it was no longer confined to Enlightenment infidels. Bolstered by German and French scholarship, pastors fresh from divinity school could tell their congregations that the Book of Isaiah was written by several people, none of whom was named Isaiah. In other words, higher criticism undermined faith in the Bible as God's word *in any simple sense.* If pastors tended to discuss these twin challenges gingerly after wrestling with their own doubts, Robert G. Ingersoll and his fellow militant agnostics bluntly told surprisingly large audiences that religion was an unscientific delusion.

These challenges produced a split within Protestantism that ultimately widened into a chasm. Theological liberals adapted to intellectual modernity. Accepting higher criticism, they were skeptical of Old Testament history and New Testament miracles. The "days" of creation in Genesis might have stood for millions of years of evolution; perhaps Jesus himself was only an admirable mortal rather than God's divine son. Similarly, biblical references to the coming kingdom of God could be read as admonitions to build a good society here and now rather than as predictions of Jesus' eventual return. Forsaking the notion of original sin, most liberals believed that mankind was moral enough to create a good society. Finally, though theological liberals were not so oblivious to evil as fundamentalist and neo-orthodox critics maintained, they generally embraced the prevailing idea of progress.

In all essentials, theological conservatism was the opposite of theological liberalism. The Bible, perhaps marred by mistranslation, nonetheless remained God's word, "inerrant" in the original texts and accessible to all. God's son, Jesus, died to atone for humanity's sins. God's kingdom was no metaphor for protective tariffs or social work; rather it was a sinless world to be established after Jesus' Second Coming. Contemporary men and women, as sinful as Adam and Eve, could not make this world substantially better. Indeed, theological conservatives expected conditions to worsen until Jesus returned.

The gross differences are unmistakable. Yet especially because theological conservatives are so often misunderstood, we must appreciate some of the shadings. For example, theological liberals were not necessarily political liberals. An unsympathetic Henry Ward Beecher told striking railroad workers in 1877 that they could support their families on one dollar per day, a sum sufficient to buy bread and water. On the other hand, as the career of William Jennings Bryan demonstrates, theological conservatives were not necessarily political conservatives. Theological liberals differed among themselves in matters of doctrine as well as social policy, with many continuing to accept some biblical miracles and Jesus' divinity. Theological conservatives were more diverse than their liberal rivals in background and belief. Their ranks included urbane Calvinists, traveling evangelists, and grassroots participants who believed that conversion brought a "second blessing," including the power to heal and the gift of glos-

solalia. Veterans of this turn-of-the-century holiness revival, usually poor and demonstrative, formed Pentecostal churches, generally
shunned by more polished theological conservatives.

Some theological conservatives accepted an interpretation of
Scripture called premillennial dispensationalism. According to this
framework, which is anything but simple literalism, history was divided into eras—dispensations—in which mankind made and then
broke covenants with God. Humanity now lived in the penultimate
period to be marked by another broken covenant, the rise of Satan's
helper, the Antichrist, a great Tribulation testing all Christians, and
finally Jesus' return. Dispensationalists found in Scripture proph-
ecies of current events and they studied world affairs for evidence of
the impending Second Coming; before his ignominious departure
from Paris, Napoleon III looked like the most promising candidate
for Antichrist. Scholars still disagree about the prevalence of dispensationalism among theological conservatives in the late nineteenth and early twentieth centuries, yet its long-term significance
cannot be denied. In the 1980s, Jerry Falwell, Pat Robertson, and Hal
Lindsey proffered dispensationalist interpretations of contemporary
events to millions of Americans.

By 1900, theological liberals had captured most of the major seminaries, pulpits, and publications. As controversies at Union Theological Seminary in New York City show, this institutional dominance
was not easily achieved. Founded by Congregationalists and Presbyterians, Union became fully independent and interdenominational
after liberal Professor Charles Briggs was charged with heresy and
barred from the ministry by Presbyterian conservatives. The two
camps continued to jockey for position within Protestantism during
the Progressive era. Conservatives found new leaders, including the
staid Baptist, William Bell Riley of Minneapolis; issued the *Schofield
Reference Bible*, which brought dispensationalist exegesis to a mass
audience; and effectively argued their case in *The Fundamentals*, a
series of booklets that reached at least three million readers. Both
sides increasingly considered denominational differences less significant than the cross-denominational split between theological liberals and conservatives. During the Progressive era, however, the
split was not yet a chasm. Liberals and conservatives sometimes

cooperated on a day-to-day basis, both sides usually supported Prohibition and other purity crusades, and neither was immune to nativism. Indeed, Congregationalist social gospeler Josiah Strong wrote *Our Country*, the best-selling nativist tract at the turn of the century.

More than any other single event, World War I turned the Protestant intramural split into a chasm. Wartime fears nurtured by the Wilson administration made tolerance a rarity. With notable exceptions—Quakers, Mennonites, Jehovah's Witnesses, and radical social gospelers—Protestants, Catholics, and Jews participated in the wartime Hun Scare. For theologically conservative Protestants, the war had special significance. Most obviously, it made a mockery of facile liberal optimism. For premillennial dispensationalists, moreover, the British capture of Jerusalem in 1917 and subsequent promise of a Jewish homeland seemed to fulfill the biblical prophecy that Jews would return to Palestine shortly before Jesus' return. Dispensationalists sponsored a series of conferences to consider such remarkable events and at one such conclave in 1919 founded the World Christian Fundamentals Association (wcfa) under the leadership of William Bell Riley. In 1920 these clergy and laymen, widely recognized as a growing militant movement, were labeled fundamenta*lists* by the sympathetic Baptist editor Curtis Lee Laws.

The fundamentalist movement of the 1920s was neither monolithic nor congruent with all Protestant theological conservatives. As with any mass movement, there were internal disputes and shifting alliances. The wcfa still looked askance at Pentecostals and recruited few activists from the fiercely independent Southern Baptist Convention. Dispensational premillennialism was not yet *de rigeuer.* Contrary to cosmopolitan stereotypes, leading theological conservatives were not necessarily flamboyant. Sometimes they were prim and even erudite. None was smarter than J. Gresham Machen of Princeton Seminary. In *Christianity and Liberalism* (1923), he politely charged liberal Protestants with false advertising. By repudiating biblical miracles and the divinity of Christ, Machen wrote, liberals had moved so far from their historic faith that they could not honestly call themselves Christians.

To be sure, there were flamboyant theological conservatives. Perhaps the greatest misfortune to befall fundamentalism was to attract national attention during the 1920s, the first great decade of American ballyhoo. News media sought the sensational while those fundamentalists with a flair for publicity played to their strength. Billy Sunday, a former baseball player, agreed with Machen that liberalism differed qualitatively from Christianity, but put the case more bluntly: "Going to church doesn't make a man a Christian any more than going to a garage makes him an automobile." Almost in the same league was New York City's foremost fundamentalist, John Roach Straton of the Calvary Baptist Church. He succinctly stated the social case against Darwinism: "Monkey men means monkey morals." Discussing his home town in the apocalyptic atmosphere of 1918, Straton wondered, "Will New York be destroyed if it does not repent?" We need not belabor this sermon's answer.

The fundamentalist controversy of the 1920s occurred on two levels. On one level, the struggle escalated among Protestants to define orthodoxy and control denominational policy. The bitterness of the fight, which especially racked the Presbyterian church, can be seen in the controversial career of a prominent Baptist New Yorker, Harry Emerson Fosdick. In 1918 Fosdick, perhaps the most esteemed American preacher, became pastor of the First Presbyterian Church on Fifth Avenue. A liberal who defined God as the "creative reality," Fosdick tried to rally his fellows against fundamentalism. They in turn questioned his orthodoxy, and in 1923 the Presbyterian General Assembly launched an investigation. Although the New York Presbytery defended Fosdick, he moved to a Baptist pulpit and then in 1931 became founding minister of the nondenominational Riverside Church. During this tumult, Straton compared Fosdick to Jesse James. No rhetorical slouch himself, Fosdick called Jasper Massee, his fellow Baptist and Boston's premier fundamentalist, an "egregious ass."

Despite many such bitter remarks, the fundamentalist controversy of the 1920s would be little remembered if it had not spread beyond devout and divided Protestants to the wider culture. Although fundamentalists also battled strong drink, sexy movies, and birth control, it was the trial of John Thomas Scopes for teaching evolution that served—and continues to serve—as the preeminent symbol of their impact on American life. They had never liked Darwin's theory, but the danger seemed especially great in the 1920s. With growing high school enrollments, many more students learned about evolution, and the much-publicized "revolution in morals" convinced fundamentalists that talk of "monkey men" had indeed produced "monkey morals." Moreover, wartime bans on the German language had suggested a strategy; the possibility of barring evolution from public schools. The World Christian Fundamentals Association adopted this issue as a central concern and President William Bell Riley convinced William Jennings Bryan to lead the attack. In February 1922, the *New York Times* outlined Bryan's standard fundamentalist case against evolution. According to Bryan, evolutionary theory was not science but "Darwin's guess." It threatened religious faith by destroying belief in Jesus' virgin birth and other miracles. Finally, Bryan circumspectly suggested that Darwinism undermined proper personal morality.

Fundamentalists campaigned to bar the teaching of evolution from the public schools in at least twenty states. Straton led the unsuccessful effort in New York. But three states did ban the subject and others yielded to pressure by modifying their textbook selections. During 1925 the legislation enacted in Tennessee was challenged by John Scopes and his theologically liberal and civil libertarian allies. The defense led by Clarence Darrow wanted eminent scientists and leading liberal theologians to testify that evolution was both scientifically sound and compatible with sensible religion. When the trial judge refused to allow this testimony, Darrow called William Jennings Bryan, one of the prosecutors, to testify as an expert on the Bible. During perhaps the most famous cross-examination in American legal history, Darrow forced Bryan to admit that Scripture was often problematical and subject to divergent interpretations. A broken Bryan died within the week.

Although the Scopes trial occurred in Dayton, Tennessee, diverse New Yorkers tried to play, and some did play, major roles. The owner of a Coney Island zoo offered his prize monkey as an associate counsel for the prosecution. The offer was not accepted, but two New Yorkers, Arthur Garfield Hays of the American Civil Liberties Union and Dudley Field Malone, an iconoclastic cultural Catholic, joined Clarence Darrow in defending Scopes. Henry Fairfield Osborn of the

Museum of Natural History was recruited by the defense to certify Darwinism's scientific validity.

The Scopes trial is a flawed symbol of fundamentalism's impact partly because the issues involved are so often parodied. For example, the most accessible version of the trial, the slightly fictionalized account in *Inherit the Wind*, presents a simple conflict between science and bigotry. Yet much of the science Scopes taught was not only dubious but dangerous. The textbook he used affirmed that some products of evolution, notably Anglo-Saxons, were superior to others, notably blacks and Asians. The prospective defense witness Henry Fairfield Osborn agreed, having written the foreword to Madison Grant's pernicious nativist tract, *The Passing of the Great Race*. Moreover, Bryan pressed two points usually lost in recollections of the trial. If Friedrich Nietzsche's ideas had moved young men to murder, as Darrow had argued in his defense of Nathan Leopold and Richard Loeb, how could he then deny that Darwin's ideas could corrupt adolescents? And did not the citizens of Tennessee have the right to decide what their children learned in public schools?

There are convincing liberal and constitutional answers to these questions. Separation of church and state is a worthy though elusive goal and children should have the right to learn things their parents dislike. Yet few cosmopolitan intellectuals have appreciated, let alone addressed, the complex ethical issues latent in the first fundamentalist controversy. One who did, at least occasionally, was a native New Yorker, Walter Lippmann. In *New York World* editorials, Lippmann compared Scopes to the persecuted Galileo. Nor did he sympathize with "these millions of semi-literate, priest-ridden and parson-ridden" voters. Even so, reflecting broadly on the fundamentalist controversy, he found the Protestant modernism exemplified by Fosdick less forthright and intellectually rigorous than the conservative case made by Machen.

Ridicule, a more frequent cosmopolitan reaction to fundamentalism, was used effectively by Sinclair Lewis. After touring the hinterland in search of clerical hypocrites, Lewis settled into a New York hotel to finish writing *Elmer Gantry*. Gantry was partly modeled on John Roach. Reviewing the novel for the *New York Post* in 1927, Straton condemned Lewis's "disordered" mind and denied that there "was such a man as Elmer Gantry." Straton's side lost the cultural battle. Except among theological conservatives themselves, the picture of fundamentalism drawn by Lewis, H. L. Mencken, and fellow debunkers became standard fare.

Contrary to convention, the fundamentalist movement of the 1920s did not die with Bryan. In 1928 theological conservatives formed part of the broad band of Protestants opposing the election of Alfred E. Smith because he was a Catholic. To Southern Methodist Bishop James Cannon, a mild theological conservative but avid prohibitionist, the Democratic presidential nominee represented the "kind of dirty people that you find today on the sidewalks of New York"; New York City itself was "literally Satan's seat." Protestant defections cost Smith several traditionally Democratic southern and border states. Yet many fundamentalists did vote for Smith, considering his New York accent, hostility to Prohibition, and Catholic faith less significant than his farm program or his party's commitment to racial segregation.

The Great Depression, which began a year after Smith's defeat, was more than an economic crisis. Instead of evaporating, those cultural issues that had disrupted American life during the 1920s persisted in a less prosperous context. Some were soon resolved; for example, Democratic victories in 1932 doomed Prohibition. Others were evaded by shrewd politicians; building his remarkable coalition, Franklin D. Roosevelt won votes from most "priest-ridden" Roman Catholics and "parson-ridden" theological conservatives. Still other issues retained emotional power; many fundamentalist clergy, viewing the Depression as God's punishment for the decadent twenties, prayed for a revival rather than an economic recovery.

The Depression and New Deal moved some fundamentalists to become activists on the political far right. During the 1920s, Rev. Gerald B. Winrod had been a second-rank leader in the World Christian Fundamentals Association. Initially suspicious of Roosevelt for pushing repeal of Prohibition, Winrod by 1933 had convinced himself that the New Deal represented an agency of a vast international Jewish conspiracy against Christian civilization. He took seriously the anti-Semitic forgery, *The Protocols of the Learned Elders of Zion*, which he regarded as a sort of supplement to biblical prophecy.

Indeed, he remained a devout fundamentalist even as he became an avid anti-Semite. According to Winrod, the resemblance between the multiarmed Beast of Revelation and the multifeathered blue eagle of the National Recovery Administration illustrated the New Deal's satanic affinities.

Like social gospelers on the opposite side of the theological and political spectrums, fundamentalist far-right agitators remained a minority. Most theologically conservative clergy spent the Depression tending to their congregations. Not only did they preach and pray for revivals, but they expanded the fundamentalist infrastructure, founding magazines, Bible colleges, and summer camps. Some joined Rev. Charles Fuller of "The Old Time Revival Hour" in making effective use of radio. Cosmopolitan intellectuals, many of whom had moved to the left, paid scant attention to such prosaic activities. Rather, they focused on Winrod and his fellow far-right activists whom they usually regarded as native fascists. Nowhere was the exaggerated fear of a domestic fascist triumph greater than among New York's liberals and radicals. In the context of this Brown Scare, fundamentalists looked like a serious national threat instead of a perplexing local annoyance.

Cosmopolitan clichés about fundamentalists—originally disseminated by debunkers during the 1920s and by the political left during the 1930s and 1940s—were incorporated into social science during the 1950s. We return, then, to city college's noted alumni, Professors Bell, Lipset, and Glazer who, along with many other prominent post–World War II intellectuals, were nurtured as young men in the political culture of the New York left (currently immortalized in countless bitter, sweet, and bittersweet memoirs). There they had learned to distinguish among Stalinists, Trotskyists, and Lovestoneites without a scorecard; subsequently even their most engaged writing about the left recognized the importance of such divisions as well as the power of ideas—"ideology"—during the Great Depression. On the other hand, the political culture of New York radicalism had rendered them ill-prepared to understand the complexity of American Protestantism. When they wrote about the right, "fundamentalism" served as a catch-all synonym for moralism and reaction rather than as a name for a coherent movement marked by internal divisions and complicated relations with Pentecostals or theological liberals. Reducing theological conservatives to crude sociological categories, Bell, Lipset, and Glazer also ignored the impact of ideas. Apparently, dispensational premillennialism did not even qualify as ideology. This pluralist scholarship reflected the assumptions of the 1950s as well as the legacies of the 1930s. Sharing the prevailing belief that society was growing increasingly secular, Bell, Lipset, and Glazer naturally regarded unfamiliar, fervent religiosity as a sign of reaction.

Curiously, the pluralist view of fundamentalism as a vestigial element in the body politic won wide acceptance among cosmopolitan intellectuals, this during a decade marked by an extraordinary religious revival in which theological conservatives played a prominent part. Instead of fading away, fundamentalism was largely transformed into "evangelicalism," a transformation best symbolized by Billy Graham, still our foremost evangelical. Graham's fundamentalist origins are unmistakable. He had been converted as a youth by Mordecai Ham, attended Bob Jones University and Wheaton College, and was chosen by the aging William Bell Riley to head his Minneapolis religious empire. As late as 1955, Graham criticized *Life* magazine for accepting Darwinism. By the late 1950s, however, the changes looked more significant than the continuities. Graham was not only more polished than Riley or Winrod but also less strident. Though convinced of Jesus' ultimate—perhaps imminent—return, he named no candidates for Antichrist from the list of European statesmen. Minimizing theological differences, Graham shunned anti-Semitism, reached out to Pentecostal preacher Oral Roberts, and never compared the papacy to the biblical whore of Babylon. Wary of a Roman Catholic president, he nonetheless behaved better than theological liberals Norman Vincent Peale and Daniel Poling when John F. Kennedy sought the office in 1960.

In 1957 Graham brought his crusade to New York City, saying that he was prepared to be "crucified" in this capital of cosmopolitanism. The closest thing to a driven nail came from Union Theological Seminary. To neo-orthodox theologian Reinhold Niebuhr, Graham's pietism, lacking even the minimal realism of the social gospel, offered a "blandness which befits the Eisenhower era." On the other hand, Niebuhr's colleague Henry P. Van Dusen supported Graham's popularization of the gospel. So did the New York Protestant Council of Churches, which officially sponsored Graham's effort. Indeed, far from being crucified, Graham was lionized by New Yorkers as diverse as Ogden Reid, Henry Luce, Ed Sullivan, and Walter Winchell. The crusade lasted ninety-seven days.

If Professors Bell, Lipset, and Glazer had taken account of Graham's popularity, they might have concurred in Niebuhr's critique but drawn a different moral. Perhaps they would have discerned that bravura radicalism had become a hollow shell even among most Protestant theological conservatives who, along with their worldly counterparts, were dealing with technical problems—organizing revivals, for example—instead of dreaming chiliastic dreams. In short, they probably would have concluded that fervent fundamentalism also could be absorbed into the American religious and political consensus.

They would have been partly and temporarily correct. As Professor William G. McLoughlin wrote, Graham's New York campaign was a broad "pep rally" for Americanism. Yet Graham, Carl Henry of *Christianity Today*, and their fellow moderating evangelicals did not constitute all of the theological right. As Graham attracted national attention while moving toward the religious center, Jerry Falwell, a fundamentalist separate Baptist, began to build the Thomas Road Baptist Church in Lynchburg, Virginia. Nor need we look below the Mason-Dixon line for embryonic signs of the second fundamentalist controversy that would erupt in the 1970s. While Graham filled Yankee Stadium, Pat Robertson sat under a Modigliani print in his living room on Staten Island, sipping Courvoisier with his Catholic wife, and searching for the meaning of life he would ultimately find in a politically conservative Pentecostal ministry.

This point deserves emphasis since in some respects the religious and political situations in the late 1980s resembled those of the late 1950s. Once again, Protestant theological conservatives, recently regarded by cosmopolitans as a serious threat to the American way, are losing influence on the national scene. Major spokesmen for the theological and political right have been indicted (Jim Bakker), disgraced (Jimmy Swaggart), defeated (Pat Robertson), or worn down (Jerry Falwell). In this environment, cosmopolitan commentators again presume that current social stability will persist indefinitely and predict that noisy fundamentalists are finally fading away. Yet disappearance from the front page of the *New York Times* does not necessarily mean disappearance from American life. And the present embattlement of a grassroots movement does not necessarily preclude future resurgence. Despite many prior obituaries, the culture of theological conservatism has not only survived but has also intermittently thrived by adapting to social circumstances, recruiting fresh adherents, and producing powerful new leaders.

And it may someday thrive again.

3

Revelations: The Future of the New Christian Right

STEVE BRUCE

This chapter will consider the significance of the new Christian right, summarize its strengths and weaknesses, and speculate on the future of the sort of conservative Protestant politics it represents. One way of framing a picture of the NCR is to consider two words that often appear in explanations of it: revival and reaction (Peele 1984).

Revival or reawakening can be taken in two senses: as referring either to the Christian Church as a whole and thus to an addition of numbers to the body of the saved; or as referring only to the "faithful," thus implying a new sense of vitality. Evangelicals, and people writing about evangelicals, usually use the term to suggest a period of widespread conversion, during which new members are being added to the churches. When used in discussions of the new Christian right, it suggests that the explanation for the movement lies in the increasing popularity of evangelical Protestantism. Many discussions of the NCR begin by placing the movement within the context of the decline of the mainstream Protestant churches and an increase (relative or absolute, depending on the author) in the numbers belonging to evangelical, pentecostal, and fundamentalist churches.

Although there is something in the observation that the rise of the NCR follows the decline in the size and confidence of the main-

38

stream churches—and hence is related to the increase in confidence of conservative Protestants—it would be misleading to imply that the politicization of some conservative Protestants was a *natural* consequence of an increase in their numbers. Insofar as any connection can be discerned, it is almost the opposite; the expansion of the milieu has been accompanied by the reduction of its distinctiveness and hence of its grounds for a distinctive politics. As the claim to be "born again" has become more popular and respectable, the amount of behavioral change, of asceticism, associated with that state has been reduced. As Quebedeux signaled in the title of his book, *The Worldly Evangelicals* (1978), the gradual reduction of the amount of world-rejection involved in "getting saved"—which John Wesley observed in his upwardly mobile followers—is being repeated among American evangelicals. Hunter's 1987 study of young evangelicals shows a small but crucial change in attitudes; a relaxation in their own standards has been accompanied by an increasing unwillingness to condemn out of hand those who differ from them. Some of the certainty has gone and in its place there is an element of recognition of sociomoral pluralism. Although young evangelicals still have a strong sense of what is right for them, they no longer seem so sure that what is right for them is also right for everyone else.

There is a slight problem in interpreting these data. It might be that the expansion of conservative Protestantism has produced some relaxation at the peripheries because people who have always been conservative Protestants are less willing to forgo the pleasures their increasing prosperity is now making available to them.[1] Alternatively, it could be that the expansion has meant the incorporation of newcomers who wish some of the rewards of being born again without making what were previously mandatory sacrifices. Either way, the increasing self-confidence of conservative Protestantism has been accompanied by a relaxation of standards. This incipient pluralism and moderation offsets much of the advantage of self-confidence. Conservative Protestants may have had their morale boosted by having Jimmy Carter, a born-again Baptist lay preacher, as president, but he acted like a liberal.

The point will be pursued shortly but here it is enough to say that the simple connection of conservative Protestant revival and increased politicization assumes too monolithic a view of conservative Protestantism. A good part of conservative Protestant growth is associated with decline in the conservative elements.

The term "reaction" is often used for two distinct purposes. Sometimes it identifies a general shift to the right in American politics; sometimes it identifies the NCR as a reaction on the part of a particular section of the American people. Taking the first possibility, the political mobilization of some conservative Protestants is seen as simply one element of a general shift to the right in American politics and culture. In this scenario, Nixon's rout of McGovern, and Reagan's victories in 1980 and 1984 are evidence of a general move away from the liberalism of the Kennedy era and Johnson's Great Society; and the election of Jimmy Carter in 1976 is the exception explained by Nixon's Watergate disgrace. The idea that America has shifted to the right is one that has widespread currency, even among liberals. Especially since 1980, a significant number of younger Democratic politicians have seen it as their task to reconstruct the party to accommodate this new conservative mood.

There is actually little clear evidence for a general and significant shift to the right. In a lengthy analysis, Ferguson and Rogers (1986) persuasively argue that opinion poll data from the 1960s to the present show little evidence for a rightward shift in public thinking. For example, on attitudes toward business, support for government regulation of company profits actually *increased* between 1969 and 1979. The percentage of people thinking that business as a whole was making "too much profit" rose from 38 percent to 51 percent.

> Over the period 1971 to 1979 the percentage thinking that "government should put a limit on the profits companies can make" nearly doubled, rising from 33 to 60 percent. . . . As the rollback in regulation and cutbacks in domestic spending became evident during Reagan's first term, the public increased its support for regulatory and social programs. (Ferguson and Rogers 1986:44–45)

Nor is there any great evidence of a move to the right on sociomoral issues. An ABC poll found that support for abortion on demand, no matter what the reason, had increased from 40 percent in 1981 to 51 percent in 1985, while the percentage opposed to abortion on demand had gone down from 59 percent to 46 percent. On the issue of affirmative action, the Reagan era has seen a rise in the percentage of people declaring themselves in favor of a "federal law requiring affirmative action programs for women and minorities in employment and education, provided there are no rigid quotas" (Ferguson and Rogers 1986:46). Given the excellent opportunities for divergent readings of these sorts of questions, one would be unwise to use the considerable amount of poll data Ferguson and Rogers have amassed to argue that Americans have become conspicuously more liberal, but it is certainly difficult to find any reason—except for the election of Reagan, that is—to suppose that they have become more conservative.

Two minor points should be made about Reagan's popularity. First, even in his "landslide" of 1984, he won only 59.6 percent of the votes cast; 40.4 percent went to Mondale. Gallup regularly records presidential popularity ratings. Over the four years of his first term, Reagan's rating was 50 percent, which, as Ferguson and Rogers note, was *lower* than that of Eisenhower (69 percent), Kennedy (71 percent), Johnson (52 percent), and Nixon (56 percent), and not much above that of Carter (46 percent). Reagan's rating peaked shortly after taking office, when 68 percent of those polled approved of his performance. Eisenhower (79 percent), Kennedy (83 percent), Johnson (80 percent), and Carter (75 percent) had higher peaks, while Nixon's 67 percent was not significantly lower. The second point is that, as Ferguson and Rogers plausibly argue using correlations with economic indicators and poll data, Reagan's popularity and election victories are for the most part simply explained by the performance of the economy. The weakness of the economy cost Carter the 1980 election, and its strength in 1984 won Reagan a second term.[2]

Put briefly, there is little reason to suppose that there has been a major shift to the right. Furthermore, even those analysts who see a move to the right on economic issues add that there has been no corresponding shift on sociomoral issues. Haynes Johnson, a Pulitzer prize-winning journalist who has been writing about American politics for over thirty years, said that

> the real revolution in America is not a political but a personal one. By that, I mean a revolution in personal attitudes and values—sexual and racial primary among them. These changes in behavior and attitudes, startling when compared to the more straightlaced traditional America of

> a generation ago, also hold significant political implications. We have today, if I'm right, a citizenry that is far more liberal in terms of its social values—favoring abortion, much more tolerant about sexual behavior, about divorce, about racial relations and civil rights—and yet also notably more conservative when it comes to fiscal and governmental matters, especially government from Washington. (in Duke 1986:39)

Even those who are Reaganite on the handling of the economy, defense, and foreign policy wish to maintain the freedom to choose their own lifestyles.

The second reading of "reaction," which sees the NCR as a reactionary political movement supported by a section of the population that feels itself threatened, is more plausible. However, the notion of reaction has to be used carefully if it is not to mislead. We should not see the NCR as an almost neurotic response to social, political, and cultural changes which threaten small-town Americans and their traditional values. Those analysts who have tried to deploy status defense models of the NCR have usually had to admit that they do not work (Simpson 1983, 1985; Buell 1983). Unless status is defined so broadly as to be meaningless, supporters of the NCR do not share a common status. Apart from a tendency to be located in the South or Southwest, the main thing that supporters of organizations such as the Moral Majority have in common is their religion. The NCR is a movement of cultural, rather than status, defense. To use the American phrase, it is concerned with the politics of lifestyles rather than status.

The word "reaction" also has the unfortunate suggestion of bad faith about it; it implies that while liberals have authentic values, which they hold dear for good reasons, their opponents take up positions in reaction. The core of conservative Protestant values has remained remarkably stable for a long time. The social, political, and moral conservatism of evangelicals and fundamentalists is not new. They have not become conservatives in response to the increasing permissiveness of liberal America. They have stood still while everyone around them moved. If liberals see the conservative movement as a reaction, this is akin to the illusion of children in a train that is leaving the station supposing that they are standing still while the stationary train next to them is moving backwards.

What is novel or reactive about the actions and attitudes of people like Falwell, Robertson, Dixon, and their followers is their willingness to campaign publicly and politically against things they find offensive. Although fundamentalists have always found something to complain about—after all, this world is the world of fallen and sinful man—their environment has grown increasingly hostile. The unregenerate part of the world has become ever more obviously unregenerate. One need not follow fundamentalists in their uncritical attitude to the past, their blanket condemnation of the present, nor in their explanation of the ways in which the world has changed to accept that divorce is now common, as is drug addiction, that homosexuality is accepted in many circles as an alternative lifestyle, that "housewife" is a devalued status, that the separation of church and state (once interpreted as denominational neutrality) is now taken to imply secularity, and so on. The changes that have been promoted and welcomed by atheists, feminists, racial minorities, and liberals are changes that have fundamentally altered the moral, social, and political culture of America and moved it away from the standards and practices that fundamentalists regard as biblical.

Furthermore, and probably more important, the changes in American culture have been accompanied by a social force that amplifies the offense to conservative Protestants: increased centralization. Although America remains far less centralized than Britain, the general trend has been in the direction of increased cultural and economic penetration of the peripheries and increased government intervention in the lives of individuals. I suggest that increased intrusion is more important than increased liberalism because it is the "proximity" of what offends that defines the extent of the offense. Conservative Protestants always knew that people in Los Angeles or New York were desperate sinners, but so long as they could live in their own shared and socially constructed subsection of America, it was not something that really hurt.

Some subsocieties and subcultures are geographical; they are regional peripheries, backwaters, or "ghettos." Others are social constructions which can, with effort, be sustained in the "centers" of modernity. However, in either form, such subcultures depend on structural conditions permitting their survival. Conservative Protestants felt themselves pushed into political action because they saw the state making increasing demands on them. They used to have racially segregated schools which began the day with public prayers. Racial integration is now public policy and the courts enforce a strict separation of church and state. Conservative Protestants react by establishing their own independent Christian schools. The state then intervenes again, depriving those which appear to be segregationist of their tax-exempt status and supporting those state legislatures that require the licensing even of independent schools. It is this sense of having their autonomy reduced which explains the considerable hostility to cosmopolitan America. This point is important in responding to Miller (1985) and others who wish to deny the novelty of the new Christian right. The sense of grievance which led to the mobilization of the NCR is qualitatively different from early conservative Protestant political movements. The rejection of liberal cosmopolitanism is common to the fundamentalism of the 1920s and the 1970s, but the replacement of world communism by secular humanism as the bogeyman represents an important change. Communism was "out there" somewhere. Although fundamentalist leaders such as McIntire and Hargis (Forster and Epstein 1964) followed Senator McCarthy in seeing signs of communist infiltration in the heart of American institutions, communism was always a somewhat remote threat. The most recent wave of fundamentalist politicization is a response to changes that need very little social construction to appear to be just beyond the glow of the campfire.

Increasing secularity and liberalism could have been ignored by fundamentalists so long as they were permitted the social space in which to create and maintain their separate social institutions. Unfortunately for them, it is in the nature of modern industrial societies to reduce that social space.

There is nothing new about such boundary disputes. Many previous contests have occurred between particular religious minorities and the state. The Mormons were forced to abandon polygamy. Jehovah's Witnesses and Christian Scientists have come into conflict with the state over their refusal to permit such medical interventions as blood transfusions. In most states some sort of accommodation has been achieved, with religious exceptions to general laws being permitted. But what distinguishes the Mormons, the Witnesses, and the Christian Scientists is that they were despised minorities who were pleased to be tolerated and who had no great imperial ambitions. What makes the recent church-state conflicts serious is that they involve a very large minority that has imperial ambitions. Not surprisingly, given that their beliefs and values, language and thought once dominated very large parts of America, conservative Protestants want to see themselves as a moral *majority*.

To summarize, the people whom Jerry Falwell represents have not grown dramatically in numbers in the last fifteen years, although their ability to utilize new technology has raised their public profile. Liberals had simply forgotten that large numbers of people did not share their beliefs and values. The cosmopolitans and intellectuals who supervised the media and ran the bureaucracies of the major denominations had concentrated on the struggles for the rights of women and blacks, on the student movement, and on the protests against the Vietnam War, and neglected the American conservative Protestant. It is not so much fundamentalism but *public awareness* of fundamentalism that has been born again. Insofar as some element of growth was involved in the rise of the new Christian right, it was the growth of evangelical and fundamentalist self-confidence, part of which came as an incidental feature of the rise of the sunbelt.

Similarly, the increased politicization of fundamentalism should not be seen as a reaction, if by doing so one implies that it is fundamentalists who have changed markedly. Insofar as there is a reactive element, it is not in the beliefs and values of fundamentalism but in the subculture's recognition that, to hold what it had and to avoid losing more, it must actively resist. If one is looking for a single word to describe the rise of the new Christian right, then "reassertion" would be appropriate.

Fighting Back

Fundamentalists are moved to fight back, either by changing the content of liberal and cosmopolitan culture or, more typically, by resisting the incursions of that culture and demanding the right to social space. I have tried to show that such resistance has a series of ironic consequences. To have any chance of success, it must concede many of the things fundamentalists wish to preserve. When the concessions are not made, the NCR's claim to being a serious political movement is undermined. Given the smallness of the conservative Protestant population and its regional concentration, realistic political action requires pragmatism and accommodation. To have any hope of maintaining the social practices they believe their religion requires, fundamentalists must compromise what is distinctive about that religion. In the world view that creates the particular reasons conservative Protestants have for resisting modernism, Catholics and Jews are not Christians, and Mormonism is a dangerous cult. But legislative and electoral success requires that fundamentalists work in alliance with such groups and with secular conservatives.

The final irony of the position of contemporary fundamentalists is revealed in their attitude toward minority rights. Fundamentalists object to the language of group rights, first because their religious and political ideologies are constructed around individualism, and second because the groups—racial minorities, feminists, and homosexuals—which have so far deployed the notion of group rights represent causes that fundamentalists have to date opposed. Nevertheless, the new Christian right has been most successful in the public arena when it has presented its own cause as that of an oppressed and hard-done-by minority. As yet, this rhetoric appears only occasionally in fundamentalists' complaints about the neglect of their values and in the strategic thinking of NCR lobbyists and lawyers. But it is easy to imagine it taking hold and serving as a vehicle for coming to terms with modern America. The regionalism expressed in "states' rights" will become the pluralism of minority rights and with it will come the end of any dream of a Christian empire.

The Defeat of the NCR

It is perhaps premature to explain the failure of a social movement that has not yet died, but enough of the signs are already there—in fact, have always been there for those who wished to see them—for us to attempt an explanation.

The first point to make is that the potential support base for the NCR was always smaller than many commentators noticed. First, the movement has failed to attract the support of any significant number of conservative Catholics, Jews, Mormons, and others. But even if one confines the examination to conservative Protestants, it is clear that not all the members of those denominations which can sensibly be described as "conservative Protestant" share the religious or political beliefs of Jerry Falwell. Commentators who notice only the growth of conservative Protestantism relative to the mainstream denominations are liable to see it mistakenly as an homogeneous or coherent base for the NCR.

Consider the Southern Baptist Convention, the largest grouping of conservative Protestants. Much has recently been made of the capture of a number of key organizational positions in the convention by active supporters of the NCR.[3] One might suppose that the entire membership of the SBC can be counted as present or future NCR supporters, and journalists do make this mistake. Actually it is likely that more than half the SBC-affiliated congregations would stand apart from the NCR, either because they are sufficiently liberal to disagree with NCR positions or because, while themselves holding to such positions, they accept the right of others to disagree. A survey of the attitudes of 431 SBC pastors toward the Moral Majority showed that fewer than half were either members or supporters of the movement. Almost all the others described themselves as opponents (Guth 1983:120).

The rift between "orthodox" conservative Protestants and those who are becoming slightly more liberal is not the only important division. NCR supporters are also criticized from the separatist fundamentalist position associated with Bob Jones University and its graduates. In one of a series of pamphlets entitled *Fundamental Issues in the 80's*, John Ashbrook concludes his critique of Falwell's *The Fundamentalist Phenomenon* by arguing that Falwell has changed camps. Falwell's concern to promote social issues has led him to abandon his separation from apostasy, the touchstone of fundamentalism. Another pamphlet in the series is called *Enforced Morality Does Not Produce Revival*. Bob Jones III has clearly expressed the view of this element of conservative Protantism:

> The aim of the Moral Majority is to join Catholics, Jews, Protestants of every stripe, Mormons, etc., in a common religious cause. Christians can fight on the battlefield alongside these people, can vote with them for a common candidate, but they cannot be unequally yoked with them in a religious army or organization. Morality is a matter of religion: a man's morality is based upon his religious beliefs. . . . Alliances we would avoid at the local level are not made acceptable or less ecumenical due to the national level on which they operate. . . . A close, analytical, biblical look at the Moral Majority . . . reveals a movement that holds more potential for hastening the church of Antichrist and building the ecumenical church than anything to come down the pike in a long time, including the charismatic movement. (Bob Jones III 1980:1–3)

That there is an element of truth in Jones's assessment is suggested by Falwell's response to the crisis in the PTL ministry which followed Bakker's disgrace. Falwell is a traditional fundamentalist; PTL is a pentecostal ministry. In theory, Falwell should have regarded PTL as the purveyor of an unbiblical deceit. Instead, he pledged to do all he could both to preserve the organization and to maintain its audience, and assured its supporters that it would continue to be pentecostal. He defended this compromise of fundamentalist orthodoxy on the ground that the collapse of the PTL network would be seen by liberals and secularists as a victory. In the face of such enemies, pan-Christian solidarity is more important than doctrinal rectitude. It seems that the pragmatic accommodation originally advanced for the Moral Majority but denied for the religious sphere has spread from the political to the religious.

Conservative Protestantism is internally divided by theology and by differences over the correct way to interpret the need for "separation from apostasy." A third source of division is, to some extent, related to this second point. Conservative Protestants are also divided on the issue of legislating righteousness. Their ambivalence about imposing their morality on others who do not share their views has its roots in a genuine commitment to democracy. At points I have talked about pragmatic accommodation as if it were something distasteful which the circumstances of the American polity has forced on the NCR. While there is a certain economy in presenting the story in that manner, if left unqualified it does an injustice to the conservative Protestant tradition. Conservative Protestantism contains within it a tension between the obligation for the saints to rule righteously (even if that means imposing righteousness on the unregenerate), and the equally strong commitment to every individual's ability to discern the will of God. Although the latter tendency is theocratic rather than democratic, in practice it results in the same thing. And it is certainly the case that conservative Protestants have historically played a major part in the promotion of democracy and bourgeois individualism. It is the tragedy (in the strict sense of the word) of conservative Protestantism that one of its most valued consequences also undermines the conditions for its survival as the key source of values for a whole society rather than as the partial world view of a self-selecting minority of saints. This is the moral to be drawn from the many surveys that show ambivalence among conservative Protestants about movements such as the Moral Majority. On the one hand, conservative Protestants want to see the world "returned to biblical standards." On the other, their theology, ecclesiology, and history give them a strongly felt commitment to freedom of choice.

Some conservative Protestants choose pietistic retreat from the world on its own intrinsic merits as an alternative to imposing their righteousness on the unregenerate. For others it has been a sensible reaction to the failure of their more activist phases. The Reformed Presbyterians are a good example. In the early days of the Reformation in Scotland, the Reformed Presbyterians (or Covenanters) were the most radical "impositionists." When they failed to win over the majority of the Church, they maintained their rhetoric of the saints and the civil magistrate working in a godly harmony, while effectively retreating from the world. The American conservative Protestant tradition displays frequent alternation between periods of active involvement and retreat. Even when the activist element has been dominant there have been those who decry social and political involvement as a diversion, a waste of the energy that should be directed to the primary task of saving souls. It needs very little by way of disillusionment with the active mode to swing the pendulum back to pietistic retreat. Not being complete retreatists, the followers of

Bob Jones's position encourage Christians to be politically active but insist on maintaining such a clear separation from apostasy that concerted political action is almost impossible.

One Moral Majoritarian described fundamentalists as a "disciplined charging army" (Fitzgerald 1981). A political scientist called them "an army that meets every Sunday" (Buell 1983). It would be more accurate to see them as a motley crew of half-hearted volunteers being pressed into service just when the crops need planting, torn between joining battle with the enemy and returning to tend their farms.

Economic and Social Cleavages

Further sources of internal fragmentation derive from socioeconomic differences among conservative Protestants. Without wishing to countenance the a priori assumption of many social scientists that religious values are secondary to more concrete economic and social characteristics such as wealth and status, it is worth remembering that religious values compete with more mundane interests in the decision making of conservative Protestants. While it is certainly the case that conservative Protestants differ from their more liberal brethren in giving a higher priority to "biblical" positions, their interpretation of biblical injunctions and their willingness to act on such interpretations differ. In the period leading up to the Civil War, people with the same theology and ecclesiology developed fundamentally different attitudes toward the slavery issue, and conservative denominations divided into northern and southern branches. There may be no single secular issue likely to produce such an emotive or clear division within contemporary conservative Protestantism, but regional and status differences remain fissures which prevent conservative Protestants from thinking and acting as a coherent body. I have already mentioned the division on economic liberalism between what, for brevity, I will call North and South. Northern conservative Protestants are much more comfortable with doctrines of *laissez-faire* than are southerners, who profit considerably from government spending.

Another division concerns race. Although most conservative Prot-

estants are less likely than liberals to be supporters of racial integration, they are divided between those who are willing to support
segregationist independent schools and social action to maintain
residential segregation, and those who openly reject segregationist
views and actions.

Finally, there is the neglected but important issue of priorities.
The large number of surveys mentioned in this work (and many
others) show that religion is important as a source of political images
and decisions. We know that religion matters; what is more difficult
to know is its place in the hierarchy of concerns on which any person
draws to make a political decision. It is likely that some of the
differences in the conclusions of surveys which have tried to measure
the importance of theology or denominational affiliation are a result
of individuals reordering their priorities. Some reordering may be
caused by the questions asked in surveys. The very fact of being
asked about one thing rather than another may produce a temporary
reassessment of concerns. But it also seems likely that issues vary in
salience depending on what is going on in the immediate world of the
respondent. We can imagine conservative Protestants arranged on an
axis of orthodoxy and suppose that those at the orthodox end consistently give a higher priority to their religious beliefs and values than
do those at the liberal end. But at any point on the axis, the relative
importance of religiously rooted values will vary with the events that
impinge on their lives. While we may assume that values have a
certain enduring quality, it also seems clear that their salience varies
in response to "agenda-setting" events in the world. If abortion is a
topical issue, something which is frequently addressed and debated
in the media and which features in elections, it will remain high on
the list of priorities for those people who have strong views on the
subject. When abortion slides down the public agenda, it will also
seem less pressing for many of those who have strong views, not
because their views have changed but because there is pressure and
opportunity to address other issues.

Clearly a section of enthusiasts will strive to keep public attention
focused on their concerns, but they have to compete for attention
with enthusiasts for other causes. Insofar as any particular group of
moral entrepreneurs has only a limited ability to set political agen-

das, there will be long periods when the issues around which conservative Protestants can unite are not very high on the lists of priorities even of conservative Protestants. To take an example from early 1987, the scandal over the sale of arms to Iran and the diversion of funds to the Nicaraguan Contras caused considerable media and public attention to focus on the honesty and competence of President Reagan and his officials. There was so much interest in "Iranscam" and so many powerful forces working to keep attention focused on the general competence of the Reagan administration that NCR lobbyists found themselves and their concerns marginalized. In very simple and practical terms, they could no longer get important people on the telephone. Even their sympathizers were engaged in other matters.

The same point can be made about many of the local elections in November 1986. In many areas, NCR activists found it impossible to make "pro-family" concerns topics of interested debate. Instead most people, even many conservative Protestants, were interested in the economy. Even if the absence of NCR issues on the local political agenda did not cause potential supporters to give a higher priority to economic interests or foreign policy concerns, it almost certainly caused many to hold back from the debate and from voting. This problem is well appreciated by new Christian right activists. Much of their time is taken up, not with mobilizing support for a certain position on an issue, but with trying to make something that concerns them into a public issue.

Liberal Reaction

The exaggerations of the cohesion and commitment of the supporters of the NCR, which were characteristic of many early responses to the NCR, were often accompanied by almost total neglect of the power and influence of various liberal groups. The NCR was sometimes described as if its opposition had already been eradicated. In particular, a point of chronology that has considerable implications for the future was neglected. The organizational infrastructure of the new right and the NCR were described in terms which suggested that their sophisticated fund-raising and opinion-formation techniques were novel. Far from this being the case, until the late 1970s the majority of ideological PACs were liberal. Had the accounts of the NCR's mobilization made more of the fact that many of the movement's techniques were borrowed (even if, like direct mailing, they were considerably improved in the borrowing) from liberal causes, it might have been obvious earlier that the NCR would not have a clear run.

Although as a very general proposition liberals are more fragmented than conservative Protestants, they can form effective organizations and campaign for their goals when they feel sufficiently moved to act. With hindsight it is easy to see that much of the NCR's success was due to the element of surprise. The resolution of the Texas textbook controversy, the defeat of the Arkansas and Louisiana "equal time for creation science" bills, and the rejection of Judge Robert Bork show how effective liberals can be once they realize that they can no longer assume their views will naturally triumph but must actively promote them. In the field of electioneering, the right-wing steamroller that removed McGovern, Bayh, Church, and other liberals appeared unstoppable; but those liberals who confronted negative campaigns head-on, rather than ignoring them as beneath contempt, won and, in some cases, improved their vote.

On the national stage, People for the American Way has become a highly efficient counter to the NCR. Having raised considerable sums of money, PAW is now in a position to counter the NCR with the same sophisticated technology, as an example will show. In September 1986, Pat Robertson staged a huge rally to test the waters for a presidential election campaign. As many as 216 conference halls throughout the country were booked and satellite time was leased to telecast the rally direct to around 200,000 potential supporters. The aim of this expensive operation was to bypass the conventional news media, which Robertson supposed would be unsympathetic to his ambitions. To counter this initiative, PAW booked a second satellite and offered free to any television station in the country that wanted it, a short program of film clips of Robertson saying the sorts of things that would have been acceptable to the narrower audiences for which they were originally intended but that were potentially damaging to his new image as aspiring presidential candidate. In many of the major markets, television stations took advantage of the free PAW material and inserted parts of it into their news reports of the Robertson rally. Although stations already sympathetic to Robertson's views ignored the PAW feed, many noncommitted stations, which might otherwise have given Robertson some excellent publicity (his intention), presented a less flattering picture of the candidate. What had been designed by Robertson's organization as a good publicity return on a considerable investment was countered by an action that had the three qualities hitherto primarily associated with the NCR: imagination, good organization, and heavy funding.

Initially begun with a short anti-NCR television commercial, PAW has grown in six years to a membership of around 250,000 and a budget of $7.6 million. A weekly radio commentary on church and state issues is provided free to radio stations around the country. Staff writers produce weekly opinion pieces offered free to local newspapers, many of which are only too happy to have the free, professionally produced copy. A list of well-known public figures who will speak against the NCR is maintained so that people with appropriate expertise can be rapidly mobilized to present a liberal view on whatever is topical.

A major problem for NCR leaders is the need to alternate between two rhetorics: one designed for the faithful audience of fundamentalists, the other directed at nonfundamentalist potential allies. In his 1984 reelection campaign, Representative Mark Siljander, an adviser to Christian Voice, sent a letter to some 400 conservative pastors in his district urging them to help defeat Jewish Michigan Democrat Howard Volpe and "send another Christian to Congress." Unfortunately for Siljander, one of the conservative pastors had moved on and been replaced by a more liberal man who made sure that PAW and the press saw this evidence of religious particularism. Whereas in the first years of the NCR such disclosures were haphazard, PAW now maintains a staff of researchers who assiduously monitor the writings and sermons of Falwell, Robertson, Swaggart, and others so that the views they would prefer to express only to the inner circle of the faithful are now given wide exposure.

In addition to closely monitoring NCR leaders in order to undermine their painstakingly calculated "presentations of self" (to use

Erving Goffman's term), liberals have themselves become adept at skillful self-presentation. Alert to the damaging consequences of being seen as avowed secularists, PAW and similar organizations have stressed their support from Christians with impeccable conservative theological credentials. Three of the most prominent spokesmen in the campaign against the NCR are John Buchanan and James Dunn, both Baptist ministers, and Chuck Bergstrom, a respected conservative Lutheran clergyman. Such men have been able to argue that, far from promoting the Protestant cause, the NCR is debasing true religion. Instead of criticizing school prayer on secularist grounds, they can argue that public prayer in school trivializes their faith. With obvious conviction they can rest their case for the separation of church and state on the sentiments voiced by Justice Black in the majority opinion in the landmark *Engel* v. *Vitale* case:

> It is neither sacrilegious nor antireligious to say that each separate government in this country should stay out of the business of writing or sanctioning school prayer and leave that purely religious function to the people themselves and to those [*to whom*] the people choose to look for religious guidance. (Abrahams 1983:90)

The Spectators

Most Americans are neither committed liberals nor committed conservatives. Insofar as we can tell from the complex mass of survey data and other sources of information, there is considerable ambiguity, both in responses to NCR issues and in feelings about NCR leaders and organizations. In the end, a major determinant of the very limited success of the NCR will be the ability of fundamentalists to present themselves as a legitimate minority. To create the social space required to maintain their subcultures and subsocieties, conservative Protestants will have to convince the general public and the social groups with power and influence that they have legitimate rights which are presently being infringed, and that such rights can be accepted without significant social instability. There are problems for both actors and audience with this performance.

For the conservative Protestant now claiming to be a member of a hard-done-by group, the problem is one of muting demands. The

belief that the survival of America as a nation requires the pre-
dominance of conservative Protestant beliefs and values is still too
strong for the new mask of moderation not to slip. Changing Moral
Majority Inc., to the Liberty Federation does not stop fundamentalists dreaming of the righteous empire. It is almost asking too much of
committed conservative Protestants to expect them, in Falwell's
words, to "coalesce with fellow Americans with whom they have
theological disagreements for the purpose of effecting moral and
social change" (1986: 1). However inelegantly Falwell may put it,
conservative Protestants do not have theological disagreements with
other people. They have the truth and other people are wrong. It is
difficult for them now to deflate their self-image from that of a
"moral majority" to that of a minority which asks nothing more than
the right to do what is right in its own eyes.

The problem from the point of view of the audience is the authenticity of this new character. That many white, heterosexual, male
Americans accepted that blacks, homosexuals, and women had been
relatively disadvantaged was an important element in the limited
success these groups have enjoyed in presenting themselves as minorities deserving of first tolerance and then positive discrimination.
Conservative Protestants once played a major part in setting the
social and moral tone of the nation; they succeeded in making alco-
hol consumption illegal. They have often been in the forefront of
campaigns to prevent the extension of toleration to other groups.
They were anti-Catholic, anti-immigrant, anti-Semitic, anti-black,
anti-homosexual, and anti-feminist. Groups that have never enjoyed
power have not had the opportunity to behave badly toward others.
Hence they can appeal to fairness without having that appeal undermined by the record of their own previous actions. Conservative
Protestants once enjoyed considerable power (and are still powerful
in some regions). While their exercise of power was not consistently
malign, neither was it uniformly benign. It is easy for uncommitted
observers to be suspicious of the change of the title of Falwell's
organization. While Falwell would always have denied imperialist
and impositional ambitions, the word "majority" always carried the
sense that, even if conservative Christians were not a majority, they

would behave as if they were by imposing their views on society as a whole. Liberty Federation is more consistent with the minority rights strategy, but many spectators doubt the sincerity of the new posture.

To summarize, any balanced assessment of the NCR has to consider the internal weaknesses of the movement as well as its strengths. It must also consider the effectiveness of liberal opposition. I have suggested that the failure of the earlier grand designs for cultural reformation has led the NCR to experiment with the potentially more fruitful strategy of claiming social space for its beliefs, values, and practices on the grounds that it represents a legitimate minority against which the modern secular state discriminates. The difficulty with that rhetoric is that many other groups have good reason to remember the lack of generosity of conservative Protestants when they were in the ascendant.

Religious Particularism and Modernity: Concluding Thoughts

Twenty years from now, scholars will be in a much better position to judge the impact of the new Christian right. This study has argued that the power and influence of the movement have been greatly exaggerated, by its enemies as much as by its friends. The NCR has failed to achieve any significant legislative success, it has failed in its main goal of re-Christianizing America, and there are few reasons to suppose that it will at some future time succeed. Thus far the movement's failure has been explained in terms of complex relationships between the interests of potential NCR supporters and the circumstances in which they must work. In concluding, I want to draw attention to a more abstract concern: the problem of modernity. Underlying the particular organizational and motivational problems already discussed is the fundamental difficulty that what has brought the NCR into being is so amorphous as to be barely identifiable while at the same time being irreversible. What troubles supporters of the NCR is modernity, and it will not go away.

What is Secular Humanism?

It is not usually the job of the sociologist to correct people's apprehensions of the world. If people define situations as real, then they are, for them, real. As a dictum for explaining why people do what they do, this is excellent. But when we move from explaining action to explaining why those best-laid schemes "gang aft agley," a contrast between the way people define situations and our understanding of them is useful.

Most NCR leaders and supporters suppose that their grievances are the result of a conspiracy by an identifiable group of secular humanists. They are wrong. The Humanist Manifestos are red herrings, the credos of a small handful of not especially influential intellectuals.[4] Godless America of the 1980s is no more the creation of secular humanists than the America of the 1950s was the creation of communists. Were major social changes the result of identifiable people acting deliberately, consciously, and in concert, there would be better reasons to suppose the NCR might succeed in reversing them. A more accurate understanding of the source of the changes that disturb the NCR allows us to see the impossibility of the mission. What is required for that understanding is some notion of the distinctiveness of the modern world.

Berger et al. reasonably define modernization as the "institutional concomitants of technologically induced economic growth" (1973: 15). The most important of these are directly related to the economy, and closely related to them are "the political institutions associated with what we know as the modern state, particularly the institution of bureaucracy" (1973: 16). Many things could be said about the consequences of technology and the modernity that accompanies it; this brief description will concentrate on professionalism and pluralism.

Taking the second point first, modernity brings with it a near-inconceivable expansion of the area of human life which is open to choice.[5] Premodern man lived in a world of *fate*. In a world of only limited technology, the one tool was accompanied by a belief in the one way:

> One employs this tool, for a particular purpose and no other. One dresses
> in this particular way and in no other. A traditional society is one in which

the great part of human activity is governed by such clear-cut prescriptions. Whatever else may be the problems of a traditional society, ambivalence is not one of them. (Berger 1980: 12)

This is not to say that traditional societies are static; they do change, but their institutions—their routinized patterns of action—are marked by a high degree of certainty and "taken-for-grantedness." In most areas of life, things are done this way, and have always been done this way, because "that is how we do things." Modernity *pluralizes:* "Where there used to be one or two institutions, there are now fifty. . . . Where there used to be one or two programs in a particular area of human life, there are now fifty" (Berger 1980:15).

Pluralization brings the need for choice. In contrast to the world of fate inhabited by traditional man, in innumerable situations of everyday life modern man must choose, and the necessity of choice reaches into the areas of beliefs, values, and world views. For the modern society as a whole, pluralization requires that the state become ever more universalistic. Increased social differentiation and migration make populations less homogeneous. The gradual expansion of economies and of the state makes variations in ethnos, in religion, in race, and in language ever more troublesome. In traditional economies people trade preferentially and particularistically. In the modern capitalist economy, production and distribution are universalized. Although the process is never complete, the tendency is for modernizing societies to treat ever-larger proportions of the people in "the same way." The expansion of citizenship rights sees the universalizing of the franchise, of property rights, and of welfare provisions. The expansion of bureaucracy—the application of technological rationality to the processing of people—sees increasing slices of identity being reduced to files consisting only of data relevant to "the business in hand."

A modern democratic nation-state which contains a variety of religious, racial, and ethnic groups and which wishes to be regarded as legitimate by the bulk of its population has to push religious, racial, and ethnic particularism out of the public arena and into the private "home" world of individuals and their families. Only in the home is there sufficient consensus to prevent strongly held views and social identities being sources of social conflict. Put simply, a major consequence of pluralization is privatization.

The NCR sees the state imposing a coherent ideology which it calls "secular humanism." This is profoundly mistaken. What is actually imposed (and that term already suggests an inappropriately directed and conscious cause) is not so often the alternative dogma but the *dogma of alternatives*.

The main exceptions to this relativism occur when powerful professional groups claim dominion over some area of knowledge or action. Then the state may impose a particular view, as the Supreme Court has tacitly permitted in refusing to see creation science as a legitimate alternative to naturalistic explanations of the origin of species. However, the state endorsement of knowledge which competes with fundamentalist views is not the sole source of grievance, and it may not be the most threatening. To offer a flippant but nonetheless useful analogy, more cars are destroyed by rust than by crashes. The large obstacle that one can see is the obstacle one can avoid. As the strength of religion in Poland or the Soviet Union demonstrates, the state's attempts to produce its own functional equivalent of religion inadvertently encourages a reaction and makes it possible to continue to believe that there can be one truth, one shared vision, one world view. The *contents* of competing visions can be ignored, or considered and then rejected. What cannot so easily be ignored is the constant evidence that there are many alternative visions. In the early stages of pluralism, some of the alternatives can be dismissed by invidious stereotyping of the proponents of those views. Especially when the carriers are foreign or largely confined to a status group quite different from one's own, the alternative world views can be neutralized: Catholicism is the creed of Rome and rebellion; unitarianism and humanism are the creeds of degenerate upper classes; enthusiastic pentecostalism is the faith of the lumpenproletariat. The problem with late pluralism (to coin a parallel to the Marxists' late capitalism) is that a combination of proliferation of alternatives and social mobility makes such sanitizing-by-stereotype increasingly difficult. When there is so much variation in and across all social strata, even the most successful techniques for "cognitive insulation" fail to disguise the reality of choice.

A major task of NCR ideologues has been to present their situation as one of being persecuted. The social construction of secular humanism has been described in terms of the value it had in simplifying the many grievances into one identifiable, embodied enemy. That observation can now be extended by returning to the importance of the "two alternatives" argument used by the advocates of creation science in the Arkansas case. In that trial, and in the Alabama charge that school books taught secular humanism, fundamentalists insisted that there were only two forms of knowledge: fundamentalism and everything else. Anything not openly supportive of fundamentalism must be critical of it. It was with the purpose of reinforcing and extending that claim that the plaintiffs in the Alabama case called, as an expert witness, sociologist James D. Hunter, who argued that secular humanism was the functional equivalent of a religion. In a more detailed presentation Hunter (1986) defines humanism quite narrowly and makes the point that humanism differs from other religions in the very limited degree of consensus and coherence it engenders among its adherents. This important qualification is missed by fundamentalists. I want to go much further than Hunter and argue that the elements of humanism are so loosely articulated (in the mechanical rather than the rhetorical sense) that even his more refined presentation is misleading. For reasons that need not concern us here, I reject the value of defining religion in terms of its functions. But leaving aside the question whether humanism is a "functional equivalent" of religion, it should be clear that it does not have the consequences—in providing a *common* direction to people's lives and a *shared* world view—of, say, fundamentalism or traditional Catholicism. If humanism is defined narrowly, its support is insignificant. If it is defined broadly, as it is in the discourse of the NCR, then it is not an identifiable ideology. Instead it is the aggregation of everything that fundamentalists do not like. The social construction work of NCR ideologues is directed toward disguising that fact. The homogenizing of secular humanism and the postulation of an active group of secular humanists are useful to the NCR in arguing its minority rights case, but as a tool of social analysis they are profoundly misleading.

If one turns back to the definition of secular humanism offered by a Texan NCR organization—Pro-Family Forum—one finds that the forum objects to: (a) the questioning of fundamentalist Protestant beliefs; (b) the rejection of the possibility of a whole society sharing the same detailed moral values; (c) the tolerance of alternative sexual "lifestyles"; (d) feminism; (e) socialism; (f) government controls on business activity; and (g) dramatic medical interventions connected with birth and death. It may be possible to imagine a modern democratic society that rejected the last four. What is not possible is to imagine one that could satisfy the NCR's desire to remove the first three.

Supporters of the NCR see the rejection of their religious beliefs and their commitment to a moral orthodoxy as the work of secular humanists. Certainly secular humanists believe in the removal of religion from the public arena, in the tolerance of alternative lifestyles, and in the extension of choice. But the sociologist of modernity sees the secular humanist position as little more than the intellectual endorsement of what has already come to pass. While some of the changes that the NCR lumps under the secular humanist label have been hastened by liberal moral entrepreneurs, most are the *unintended* consequences of modernity. When even those who are conservative on economic and foreign policy matters wish to retain the right to pursue their own lifestyles, the only circumstance under which the NCR could succeed is a return to cultural homogeneity. Nothing visible to the student of the empirical social world suggests that the internal cultural fragmentation of modern societies is about to be reversed. In his analysis of the present, the sociologist thus becomes a curious bedfellow of the Bob Jones University fundamentalist; the necessary precondition for the success of the NCR is a massive religious revival. Where I differ from Bob Jones III is that I see no reason to suppose such a revival likely.

Were the grievances of American fundamentalists the result of the actions of secular humanists, they could be removed by the power of fundamentalist numbers expressed through the ballot box. After all, conservative Protestants remain one of the largest cultural minorities in America, and America is, generally speaking, a democracy. But at least part of what bothers fundamentalists is the apparent tension between items of modern scientific and technical knowledge and parts of the conservative Protestant world view. To concentrate on evolution, it may well be that a modern industrial economy can permit the survival of prescientific ideas in certain limited spheres. The ability to make missiles, launch space rockets, exploit natural resources, and competitively produce cars may not be threatened by the belief that the world is less than a million years old and was made by God in six days. However, despite the willingness of Justices Rehnquist and Scalia to leave the matter of the origins of species to the vote of state legislatures, it seems clear that the tendency of modern societies to accord priority in debates about matters of scientific interest to those with good credentials represents some sort of functional imperative, something that could not change without posing a major threat to the knowledge base of the society. If that is the case, fundamentalists are not going to win their arguments with scientists and technologists, despite the occasional minor victory.

Something similar could be said of other areas that concern the NCR. While there has been increasing hostility to the power of the professions, it still remains the case that in all advanced industrial societies, professionally accredited occupational groups dominate particular spheres of activity. Even on matters such as education, or the civil rights of the unborn or the terminally ill, where technical considerations are obviously informed by moral judgments, the opinions of professionals carry far more weight than those of lay people, largely because it is in the very nature of the modern society to translate moral and ethical matters into technical considerations (Wilson 1982: 42–52). The basic assumptions that inform modern industrial production—that all complex objects and procedures can be reduced to repeatable acts and replaceable components; that nothing is more than the sum of its parts; that everything can be measured and calculated; that nothing is sacred and that everything can be improved; that increased efficiency is the main imperative—cannot be confined to the world of work. The formal rationality which dominates that sphere gradually invades all other areas of social action. There is not the space here to present this argument in sufficient detail to convince the skeptical, but it is accepted by most sociologists (of varying ideological positions) that it is characteristic of the modern world to subordinate the moral to the technical and the lay to the professional.

My point is that the authority of professionals (especially natural scientists) is such that fundamentalists are unlikely to establish the principle that arguments such as that over the origins of the species should be settled by votes rather than by the consensus of accredited experts. Even in matters that are more commonly seen as moral and ethical rather than technical and professional, the tendency is to defer to the professionals.

But even if one does not accept these claims about the scientific and technical consequences of modernity, one cannot think away the consequence of pluralism. And, if, as I suggest, secular humanism is simply a convenient blanket term for the necessary consequences of pluralism, then clearly fundamentalists have no hope of attaining their goals because what offends them is nothing more or less than modernity itself.

Universalism and the NCR As a Legitimate Minority

The awkward position of the NCR can now be fully described by bringing the above observations about the universalizing tendencies of modern societies together with the earlier discussion of the NCR's fall-back position of presenting itself as a disadvantaged minority.

Blacks, women, and homosexuals have built their claims by pointing to the failure of parts of the economy, the polity, and the social structure to live up to the rhetoric of universalism. Far from challenging modernity, they have appealed to its core values by identifying areas in which universal principles regarding economic and political rights have not been rigorously pursued. They have presented themselves as discriminated against by the failure of the state to prevent the continuation of particularistic practices in employment, political representation, and social valuation. The demands of these minorities are thus, in theory, demands that can be met by a modern industrial society simply giving more effort to its existing dynamics. Outlawing racism and sexism can be seen as merely giving more substance to the universalizing tendency. Racist and sexist language, for example, can be eradicated by stripping the culture of certain particularistic features, by making it more bland.

The NCR's claims to the status of a legitimate minority seem quite different. NCR supporters are not disadvantaged in terms of socioeconomic status (or at least, insofar as they are, it is because of their class, region, levels of education, and other characteristics not specifically related to their shared religious culture). Where they are disadvantaged is in the status the state is willing to accord their culture. This disadvantage cannot be remedied by extending the twin principles of universalism in the public sphere and relegating particularism to the private world. It is precisely these two principles that have produced most of the changes that offend supporters of the new Christian right. Thus, although the shift from (a) aiming to re-Christianize America to (b) claiming only that their values, beliefs, and symbols be accorded due status in the public arena, is a sensible change in strategy for new Christian rightists, an understanding of the most abstract features of modernity gives every reason to suppose that it is a strategy doomed to fail.

The NCR As a Modern Phenomenon

There is a tendency to see the NCR as a reactionary movement, an outburst of resurgent traditionalism. Certainly its proponents are fond of describing it in terms such as those in the title of one manifesto: *Back to Basics* (Pines 1982). In part this characterization is appropriate but it is important also to stress the extent to which the movement has itself accommodated to modernity. This accommodation is not just a matter of adjusting rhetoric so that the religion of Creationism becomes creation science and the virtues of fundamentalism are presented, not as divine injunctions, but as socially functional arrangements. It is also a matter of conceding crucial ground to the pluralism of the modern world by accepting the need to separate religious values and sociomoral positions so that alliances can be formed with advocates of competing religious values. Leaders of the NCR insist that they have not accepted the denominational attitude (in which truth is relativized so a number of apparently and previously competing visions can all be seen as in some sense equally valid), but they have accepted another crucial element of modernity: they compartmentalize. They operate in a world of social action that has been divided into separate spheres with different values. In church, with their own people, in prayer meetings, they remain fundamentalist Protestants. But when pursuing the public agenda of sociomoral issues, they operate with a quite different set of criteria. That is, they have conceded a major part of what the modern pluralistic society demands of religion: its restriction to the private home world. Although their behavior in the public sphere is still informed by religious considerations, it is not dominated by them, and they have been diluted in order to attract maximum support from people who do not share the values and beliefs of conservative Protestantism.

The alternative to denominationalism is sectarianism: the continued insistence that what one has is *the* truth and that those who differ are simply wrong. To present the situation of religion in a modern society in the starkest possible terms, the choice is between sectarianism and denominationalism. Modernity constantly increases the costs of sectarianism. Those people who wish to maintain orthodox religious beliefs find themselves having to retreat further and further into either regional or socially constructed laagers. The NCR has tried to reduce the costs, both by seeking public support for its positions and by resisting the encroachments of the central secular state. But in trying to do those things, it has been forced to accept the denominational attitude. One can see this clearly in conservative Protestant reasoning about the possibility of a third party. Where religion exists in its "church" form, it does not need to be represented by a political party because its presence is so all pervading; Catholicism in the Republic of Ireland is a case in point. Where it exists in a sectarian form, it produces a coherent confessional party; the Calvinist antirevolutionary party in nineteenth-century Holland is an example. American conservative Protestants realize a confessional party is not a possibility. Those who talk about a religious party at all recognize that it would have to be at least a Christian or even a Judaeo-Christian party. But most of them realize that even a Judaeo-Christian party would not work; any viable third party would have to be a secular party informed by traditional (i.e., religious) values. That is denominationalism and it is a long way down the road to the point where religion is hardly a factor at all, where religiosity appears only through political attitudes that reflect general class and status interests. The situation becomes one in which the second words in the phrases "conservative Protestant," "conservative Catholic," and "conservative Jew" become redundant.

Modernity does not challenge religion. Instead it subtly undermines it and corrodes it. Fundamentalists tacitly recognize this when they refuse to be impressed or comforted by the state's willingness to permit—to *tolerate*—Mormons, Witnesses, Christian Scientists, Rastafarians, Scientologists, Moonies, and any number of more exotic religions. Although few fundamentalists say it openly, some of them recognize that it is better to be persecuted than to be tolerated as (in the language of American forms) a "religion of your preference."

Twenty or so years ago many of the sociologists who endorsed the above picture of modernity supposed that secularization—the decline of religion—was an irreversible characteristic of modern societies. Recently the sociological orthodoxy seems to have been running in the opposite direction. Although I remain committed to a version of the secularization thesis, I do not expect religion to disappear completely or quickly. And insofar as it is the broad liberal denominations that are losing support fastest, one would expect traditional supernaturalist Protestantism to become relatively more popular and influential. There is thus nothing surprising about the appearance of the new Christian right. So long as there are sizable numbers of conservative Protestants in America, there will be movement organizations that campaign and lobby on their behalf. There will continue to be skirmishes and boundary disputes. Precisely because the conflict is not between two groups of believers, but between the adherents to a coherent belief-system and modernity, it will always be difficult to judge accurately the outcome of any battle. It will depend more on counting the dead on both sides than on watching to see who marches victorious from the field. What this study has done is to consider calmly what is known about the support-base, the actions, and the impact to date of the NCR in order to evaluate the likelihood of it succeeding in its ambitions. The conclusion is that the NCR will fail—in its present form already has failed—both to re-Christianize America and to prevent further displacement of the values its supporters hold dear. And—the point made by fundamentalist critics of the NCR—the very limited successes enjoyed by the movement have been won at the cost of submitting to modernity and abandoning the ethos of orthodox separatism which has been characteristic of fundamentalism.

Afterword

Since the Moral Majority was officially chartered in June 1979, Jerry Falwell has rightly been viewed as the predominant figure in the new Christian right. On 4 November 1987 Falwell announced that he was resigning from the presidency of Moral Majority and the Liberty Federation: "I will not be stumping for candidates again. I will never work for a candidate as I did for Ronald Reagan. I will not be lobbying for legislation personally" (*Independent*, 5 November 1987). With the failure of his mission to restore the finances of the Bakkers' PTL gospel television corporation and declining income for his own *Old Time Gospel Hour*, Falwell had good reason to rededicate himself to his gospel ministry. He could take some consolation from Pat Robertson's campaign for the Republican presidential nomination. He could and did take credit for "breaking the psychological barrier that religion and politics don't mix." But no amount of brave face could alter the impression that he was leaving politics a disappointed man. Less than two years earlier, when announcing the renaming of Moral Majority, he had said:

> With the Liberty Federation, we will be advancing to another level of involvement. We will also be challenging many of our people to run for office at the local, state, and national levels. . . . We now sincerely believe that it is possible to form a coalition of religious conservatives in this nation, including the Liberty Federation and scores of similar groups, which can bring 20 million voters to the polls nationally by 1988. This is our goal. (1986: 2)

Despite those brave hopes of voter registration, the NCR failed miserably to affect the presidential succession. Though he ran an extremely well-funded and well-organized campaign, Pat Robertson made little impact and the mainstream Republican George Bush easily defeated his right-wing rivals. Robertson's candidacy was, however, extremely useful to social scientists because it produced extensive poll data which shed some light on the reasons for his defeat.

Robertson was not helped by two scandals. The exposure of the sexual misdemeanors and financial improprieties of televangelist Jim Bakker was followed by the revelation that his fellow Pentecostalist and arch-rival Jimmy Swaggart had had dealings with a Baton Rouge prostitute. At a time when Robertson was doing his best to reconstruct his biography into that of a conservative businessman whose business just happened to be religious television, the media were again able to depict televangelists as charlatans and swindlers. A good deal of the work that Falwell and others had done in persuading the public to take fundamentalists seriously was washed away in a flood of Bakker and Swaggart jokes.

But without the embarrassment of these falls from grace, Robertson would have fared hardly better. What became clear from the polls and the actual voting patterns was that even those constituencies which should have been sympathetic to Robertson were not. A September 1987 *Time* poll asked Republican voters and "leaners" who they "would be proud to have as President" and they chose as follows:

	%
George Bush	69
Bob Dole	68
Jack Kemp	58
Pete Du Pont	49
Al Haig	46
Pat Robertson	26

Not surprisingly, Robertson also came in last in questions that asked about political experience or "ability to deal with the Soviet Union"; but when asked "Is ——— someone you can trust?" respondents again put Robertson last, behind four professional politicians and a soldier! Even more significant was the distance between first and last. Bush scored an 80 percent trust rating. Robertson was trusted by only 43 percent of Republicans.

Even in the South, with its concentration of fundamentalists, Robertson was not popular. A Roper poll showed that only 16 percent of adults in twelve southern states said they would consider voting for him. What is even more important as a sign of the hostility he aroused, 69 percent said they felt negatively toward his campaign, which was the worst negative rating of all twenty potential Republican and Democratic candidates. Despite his good start in the early caucuses (where the commitment of supporters can make up for scarcity), he remained polarizing and unpopular. A poll in February 1988 showed that only 15 percent of those asked were likely to support him, whereas 72 percent said they definitely would not vote for him, a worse score than the most liberal Democrat received. The most significant poll finding concerned the intentions of self-identifying evangelical and fundamentalist Republicans. They divided 44 percent for Bush, 30 percent for Dole, and only 14 percent for Robertson. When asked if his former status as a clergyman made them more or less likely to vote for him, even conservative Protestants answered "less likely" in proportion of 42 to 25 percent. In the early days of the NCR, both critics and supporters frequently assumed that most conservative Protestants were potential NCR supporters. Slightly more sophisticated predictions of NCR support counted as actual or potential Falwellites all those who in surveys assented to anti-abortion or anti–secular humanist sentiments. What was rarely considered was the enormous difference between being generally against some phenomenon and being willing to make that issue the central focus of one's political thinking and actions. What Robertson's campaign did was to allow all those who wished to give the NCR agenda primacy over more traditional political considerations an opportunity to stand up and be counted, and the polls suggested that they were few.

The result bore out the polls. In almost every state, including his base of Virginia, Robertson came in a poor third and was beaten easily by Bush in every demographic group, including fundamentalists. What the patterns of support showed was that even most fundamentalists were happy with a division of labor; they did not want televangelists running for political office. What the progress of the campaign showed was that the more exposure Robertson got, the less popular he became.

An important part of that unpopularity was a result of organized liberal campaigning, which has also been an influence in state and local campaigns. One of the strongest suits the NCR possessed was the claim to be a victim of elite discrimination. Frequently the contrast was made between the grass roots support for NCR sociomoral positions and the unelected Supreme Court's role in maintaining liberal positions. Curiously, liberals seem to have shared the view that their positions were unpopular and there was widespread concern that changes in the composition of the Court would lead to the NCR's benefiting from the views of an undemocratic judiciary. The appointment by Reagan and Bush of four conservative justices has produced a small but important shift in the Court's position on abortion, but it is interesting that there has been no change in the Court's insistence on a separation of church and state. Furthermore, the weakening of judicial support for abortion has not produced an NCR victory. It has merely returned the issue to the political arena where contending parties have to engage in the normal business of opinion formation, electioneering, and legislative haggling. It is still early, but state and local elections between 1988 and 1991 have shown that being pro-abortion is not the electoral liability that many feared. When liberals have become aware that their positions need to be explained and defended, they have proved extremely persuasive. To put it very simply, we can conclude that the status quo does represent the general balance of view in the American public on most of the things that motivate fundamentalists to political action.

The Reagan presidency provided the NCR with its most fertile environment and it failed to have a major or lasting impact. Since Falwell retired and Robertson was humiliated at the polls, the small proportion of fundamentalists who wish to campaign on sociomoral issues have continued to do what they were doing before Falwell and his liberal critics "hyped" the movement. In those states and counties where fundamentalists are a majority, they have influence. In the rest of America, they count as simply one more small special interest group. In a culturally plural democracy, they could not be anything else.

Notes

1. This is the Niebuhr thesis (1962) for the common development of sects into denominations.

2. Although I have questioned the construction of complex variables in their research, there is less reason to challenge the responses to straightforward questions in Johnson and Tamney's Middletown study. They claim that the item most frequently chosen as "most important" from a list of issues was "inflation," and that those who chose it voted 2 to 1 for Reagan (1982: 128).

3. On recent shifts of power in the SBC, see Ammerman (1985) and *Time* (29 June 1987: 34).

4. Even Hunter (1986:6) cannot find many humanists on any narrow definition. Martin (1981: 234) says: "There can't be many true secular humanists, since only 3 percent of all Americans say that they do not believe in God, and only a tiny fraction of those belong to the American Humanist Association or to other organizations that might qualify as denominations of the 'religion of secular humanism.' "

5. This section (indeed my general sociological perspective) draws heavily on the work of Peter L. Berger and his interpretation of Max Weber and Arnold Gehlen (Berger 1973, 1979, 1980; Berger et al. 1973; and Berger and Luckmann 1973).

Bibliography

Abraham, H. J. 1983. *The Judiciary: The Supreme Court in the governmental process.* Boston.

Ammerman, N. 1985. "Organizational conflict in a divided denomination." *SBC TODAY* (December): 12–14.

Berger, P. L. 1973. *The social reality of religion.* Harmondsworth, Middx.

———. 1979. *Facing up to modernity: Excursions in society, politics and religion.* Harmondsworth, Middx.

———. 1980. *The heretical imperative: Contemporary possibilities of religious affirmation.* London.

Berger, P. L., B. Berger, and H. Keller. 1973. *The homeless mind: Modernization and consciousness.* Harmondsworth, Middx.

Berger, P. L., and T. Luckmann. 1973. *The social construction of reality: A treatise in the sociology of knowledge.* Harmondsworth, Middx.

Buell, E. H. 1983. "An army that meets every Sunday? Popular support for the Moral Majority in 1980." Paper given at Midwest Pol. Sci. Assoc. Chicago.

Duke, P., ed. 1986. Beyond Reagan: The politics of upheaval. New York.

Falwell, J. 1986. Official statement on launch of the Liberty Federation.

Ferguson, T., and J. Rogers. 1986. "The myth of America's turn to the right." *Atlantic Monthly* (May).

Fitzgerald, F. 1981. "A disciplined changing army." *New Yorker* (May).

Forster, A., and B. R. Epstein. 1964. *Danger on the right: The attitudes, personnel and influence of the radical right and extreme conservatives.* New York.

Guth, J. 1983. "Southern Baptist clergy: Vanguard of the new Christian right." In *The New Christian Right*, ed. R. C. Liebman and R. Wuthnow. Chicago.

Hunter, J. D. 1986. "Humanism and social theory: Is secular humanism a religion?" Unpublished paper.

Johnson, S. D., and J. B. Tamney. 1982. "The Christian right and the 1980 presidential election." *J. Sci. Stud. Rel.* 21:2.

Jones, B. 1980. *The Moral Majority*. Greensville, S.C.

Martin, W. 1981. "God's angry man." *Texas Monthly* (April).

Miller, W. E. 1985. "The New Christian right and fundamentalist discontent." *Social Focus* 18.

Peele, G. 1984. *Revival and reaction: The right in contemporary America.* Oxford.

Pines, B. Y. 1982. *Back to basics*. New York.

Simpson, J. H. 1983. "Moral issues and status politics." In *The New Christian Right*, ed. R. C. Liebman and R. Wuthnow. Chicago.

Wilson, B. R. 1982. *Religion in sociological perspective*. Oxford.

Catholic Integralism
as a Fundamentalism

JOHN A. COLEMAN, S.J.

Recently many major American academic conferences have focused on variant forms of fundamentalism: Islamic, Jewish, Protestant, Catholic, even Sikh. In the spring of 1988, at the University of California, Berkeley, I took part in one such symposium at which noted sociologist Robert N. Bellah startled many with his electrifying address on "Enlightenment Fundamentalism." In this presentation, he suggested that the worldwide resurgence of religious traditionalist movements (generally unanticipated by scholars a mere decade ago) came about, in part, as a reaction-formation to the narrow, scientivistic intolerance and cribbed and confined world view of the academy's positivistic fundamentalism: its exclusionary tactic of ruling out anything but what German critic Jürgen Habermas refers to as the technical-rational paradigm for understanding our world.[1] Bellah's comments alert us to the need to expand our notion of aggressive, literalist, and reductionist fundamentalisms to include scientific reductionism among our case studies.

No doubt this recent proliferation of academic conferences (and eventual scholarly volumes) on fundamentalism derives mainly from concerned foundations and funding agencies that want to understand how resurgent Islamic fundamentalism affects Middle Eastern and world politics, and that hope to fathom the new Christian right's

74

strategies for influencing the American political arena. But there is conceivably a much longer-range legitimate scholarly interest in studying variant forms of fundamentalism.

In each case, fundamentalism serves as a lens to focus on the conflict between modernity and traditionalism in divergent religious communities. The modern liberal technological project has notoriously lacked sympathy for tradition. With the exception of some social scientists, such as Edward Shils, few conceive of tradition as a universal social need and *desideratum*.[2] Few are content to view the enlightenment tradition as one tradition among many.

Fundamentalism should not be equated, *tout court*, with either traditionalism or conservatism, both of which exist in nonfundamentalist forms.[3] Indeed, fundamentalism itself is a modern phenomenon, an aggressive reassertion of elements of traditionalism in the fight against modernity. For purposes of this essay I will define fundamentalism as an innovating and aggressive form of traditionalism based on a literal and hermeneutically privileged focus of authority: a book, a set of customs, an interpreting institution such as the papacy or the Twelve Apostles in Mormonism.

Moreover, as Lester Kurtz suggests in *The Politics of Heresy*, his intriguing, award-winning book about the Catholic case of fundamentalism, case studies of fundamentalism help us understand "the social construction" of heresy versus orthodoxy as they feed off each other, dialectically, within religious traditions.[4] For, as Kurtz notes, the principal enemy of fundamentalism tends to be less an external enemy—e.g., secular humanists—than a deviant insider heretic, a stalking Trojan horse that brings the values of secular modernity into the midst of the religious camp. Thus, American Protestant invective is notoriously stronger against the National Council of Churches, and Catholic integralists decry progressive theologians within the church more than secular rationalists.

Critique of Modernity as an Erosion of Authority

I will be mainly preoccupied with the peculiarly Catholic variant of fundamentalism which in the Catholic lexicon is called *integrisme* (in French) or integralism (in German and English). Until recently, the term "fundamentalism," was not even found in French dictionaries to refer to a religious doctrine. Thus, Daniel Alexander, writing in the Belgian journal of sociology of religion, *Social Compass*, could pose the question: "Is Fundamentalism an Integrism?"[5] I maintain that integralism is the Catholic variant of fundamentalism.

At root, this Catholic version of fundamentalism does not care so much for a literalism of the book—the classic scriptural fundamentalism of Protestantism—as for "papal fundamentalism": a literal, ahistorical and nonhermeneutical reading of papal pronouncements, even papal *obiter dicta*, as a bulwark against the tides of relativism, the claims of science, and the inroads of modernity.

While we shall perceive some notable convergence between Catholic integralism and Protestant fundamentalism, we will also note distinctive differences. Since Catholicism locates authority in both scripture and tradition and reads the scripture within the living church as a "book of the church," scriptural fundamentalism does not represent, in my view, the main form of Catholic fundamentalism. At least since the papacy of Pius XII, Catholic biblical scholars employ the full apparatus of the modern historical-critical method. Moreover, the highest authorities within Catholicism have attacked biblical fundamentalism. The American bishops warned the faithful against biblical fundamentalism in their 1987 document, *A Pastoral Statement for Catholics on Biblical Fundamentalism*.[6]

Gabriel Daly, a specialist on integralism, claims that "authoritarian heteronomy can rightly be seen as the Catholic form of fundamentalism in that it treats the ecclesiastical magisterium in the same manner as the Protestant fundamentalists treat the Bible."[7] In each case, a central authority in the tradition (accepted by all in the tradition as in some sense authoritative)—the Bible in Protestantism and the papacy in Catholicism—is viewed as above history, free from every hermeneutic of suspicion, and containing a safe guide for all behavior. The authority is accepted as an all-encompassing blueprint for life. Uncritical acceptance of this authority—as the sole and inerrant authority—becomes the litmus test of orthodoxy (another term we would do well to distinguish from fundamentalism).[8]

In the late nineteenth and early twentieth century, the papacy had to meet the challenge of historical criticism and the Darwinian revolution. In so doing, it turned not to the Bible but to Catholic scholasticism (based on a Neo-Thomist revival spearheaded by Leo XIII) as its principal weapon against the historical-critical method and the scientific revolution's erosion of settled certainties. As Kurtz argues, "Much of the Modernist controversy concerned the nature of religious truth. The scholastics and Vatican authorities contended that Christian truths were universal and unchanging and that they were interpreted through the teaching authority of the church."[9]

To perceive the story of Catholic integralism as a reaction to the "modernist crisis," one must refer to the period from 1900 to 1920, focusing on the papal decree, *Lamentabili*, issued on July 2, 1907, and the encyclical, *Pascendi*, of September 8, 1907. Therein unfolds a tale of spies for orthodoxy who hounded seminary professors and Catholic writers—through the *Sapinière* group during the reign of Msgr. Umberto Benigni, Vatican secretary of state during the pontificate of Pius X. This "bureaucratic insurgency" of papal bureaucrats against an imagined cabal of scholars may at first seem to be merely an exercise in the archaic and arcane, an historical anomaly.[10] However, it set a cultural tone for much of the Catholic response to higher criticism and the scientific method, a tone that still reverberates in the Catholic world. Moreover, in the post-Vatican II church, world-wide, we see a resurgence of Catholic integralists (e.g., Msgr. Marcel Lefebvre in France, the "Tradition, Property, Family" movement in Latin America) whose journals and social stance would seem to agree with Msgr. Benigni's sour judgment: "History is one long desperate retching and the only thing humanity is fit for is the Inquisition."[11]

First, however, we need to look at the challenge of biblical fundamentalism as such (which I am arguing is not the characteristic Catholic form of fundamentalism) within Catholicism. Basically, this challenge raises two different issues: (1) the external challenge of biblical fundamentalism to Roman Catholicism and (2) the internal presence of biblical fundamentalism within Catholicism.

The External Challenge of Biblical Fundamentalism

Roman Catholicism has long been a target of opprobrium, and converted Catholics are attractive trophies for Protestant fundamentalists. The old anti-Catholic canard about "Maria Monk"-like confessions remains alive and well in the Texas-based Chick Publications, with such lurid titles as, "Who is the Whore of Revelation?", "The Beast," and "Are Roman Catholics Christians?"[12] Fundamentalist groups specializing in the evangelization of Catholics—such as Christians Evangelizing Catholics, Mission to Catholics, Inc., and Last Days Ministries—provide evangelistic tips on how to confute Catholics and show them the errors of their ways. For the fundamentalist, few conversion triumphs—with the possible exception of Jewish converts to Jews for Jesus—outshine a Catholic's conversion to fundamentalism, especially that of a priest.

Indeed, there is evidence that the long-standing Protestant fundamentalist desire to convert Catholics has been yielding dividends in the post-Vatican church. Although precise statistics are impossible to obtain, Karl Keating—who founded the defensive antifundamentalist Catholic organization, Catholic Answers—estimates that as many as 100,000 American Catholics convert each year to evangelical fundamentalism.[13] Certainly the anecdotal evidence and insider estimates from both the Catholic and the evangelical sides suggest that the number of annual converts from Catholicism to evangelical fundamentalism is sizable.

George Gallup, Jr., for example, indicates that 74 percent of America's Hispanics have been approached by evangelicals, Pentecostals, or Jehovah's Witnesses in an attempt to convert them.[14] A survey found that 10 percent of Hispanics in the archdiocese of New York had converted to another religion after migrating to the United States.

For marginal Catholics, the basic appeal of evangelical fundamentalism is similar to its appeal to mainline liberal Protestants, an appeal that Dean Kelley outlined a decade ago in *Why the Conservative Churches are Growing*.[15] American evangelicals do a much better job than mainline Protestant and Catholic churches of providing: (1) clear identity symbols of belonging to a distinctive, disciplined, and well-defined group and (2) a vivid reality of a small community of support. The modal evangelical-fundamentalist congregation, for example, contains about 180 members when compared to the modal size of a Catholic parish which numbers around 2,300 members!

In his recent book, *Catholics and Fundamentalism*, Karl Keating argues that the appeal of fundamentalism is not only to marginal, economically poor, uneducated, or young Catholics; that the bulk of Catholic converts to fundamentalism are actually middle-aged.[16] Moreover, dynamic fundamentalist groups such as Campus Crusade, the Navigators, Inter-Varsity Christian Fellowship, and the University Bible Fellowship have successfully recruited Catholic students on such campuses as Rutgers and the University of Illinois.[17]

But, I would argue, the Catholic organizational network is relatively alert and poised to answer this challenge. In their national pastoral letter on Catholics and fundamentalists, the American bishops stress that the Catholic Church is a Bible church. They encourage scripture courses at the parish level and Bible masses where, after the manner of the fundamentalists, everyone brings their well-thumbed Bibles to mass. Scripture courses abound in Catholic parishes and dioceses—almost never taught using a fundamentalist approach or hermeneutic. Moreover, conferences on the challenge of fundamentalism to Catholicism are being held throughout the country, especially in places such as Texas, Florida, and Arkansas, where the challenge is greatest. Tapes to combat the fundamentalist challenge circulate in parishes. While certain tactics of fundamentalists may sometimes be urged on Catholics, the more usual reaction echoes that of Archbishop John Whealon, who chairs the American Bishops' Committee on Fundamentalism: "I cannot understand how a Catholic could live without the mass and other sacraments, without liturgy and the Virgin Mother, without the magisterial guidance of the Lord's church."[18]

Whealon's remarks touch on the strongly sacramental imagination of Catholics. It surprises, indeed, that Catholics could be easily lured to the world view of often anti-Catholic, evangelical fundamentalists. For, indeed, when a Catholic hears the code word "the rapture," he or she is more likely to imagine some mystic state of Teresa of Avila or Catherine of Sienna than the Second Coming of Christ. The fundamentalist scholastic controversies about pre- versus postmillenialism and dispensationalism remain as arcane to most Catholics as the Catholic Tridentine disputes over transubstantiation do to fundamentalists. In any event, almost every major strand of American Catholicism—the bishops, the clergy, scripture scholars, and religious educators, even Catholic integralist groups such as the Wanderer Forum—agrees about resisting the challenge of biblical fundamentalism. Few want Catholicism to give up its sacramental and symbolic imagination to become a church whose sensibilities reflect the world of Jerry Falwell and Jimmy Swaggert.

The Internal Challenge of Biblical Fundamentalism

There exist, however, certain minor tendencies toward a biblical fundamentalism within Catholicism itself. George Gallup notes that nearly four million Catholics claim to be "born again" Bible Christians while remaining active in the Catholic church.[19] Most of these would seem to be Catholic charismatics. In the first stages of the Catholic Pentecostal movement, charismatic prayer groups held joint meetings with Protestant Pentecostals, and some leading charismatic Catholics converted out. But the history of this recent biblical fundamentalist movement within Catholicism is largely a tale of Catholic success in containing schism and constraining charism in the service of, and under the aegis of, the institutional church.

Very early on, Catholic charismatic prayer groups held their prayer meetings in the context of the Catholic mass, which emphasizes the Scriptures as a living book in the church and introduces a Catholic sensibility toward multiple and symbolic readings of the Scriptures. Moreover, shrewd chancery offices appointed nonfundamentalist priests as official diocesan liaisons or vicars to this fundamentalist-oriented movement. These tended to coopt the groups for Catholic purposes and stressed the importance of "the teaching" (a more nuanced and critical reflection period which emphasizes Catholic understandings) as a corrective to free-wheeling charismatic prayer sessions.

In a survey of Catholic Pentecostals, conducted in the early 1970s, sociologist Joseph Fichter found traces of fundamentalism and heterodox understandings, although he notes that the social attitudes of Catholic Pentecostals were much more liberal than the average for Protestant fundamentalists.[20] A later sociological study by Meredith B. McGuire, *Pentecostal Catholics,* establishes that the Catholic gamble to contain the charisma and tame the fundamentalist tendencies among Pentecostal Catholics generally paid off.[21]

McGuire documents how the new Pentecostal imagery becomes subordinated to the larger Catholic sacramental sense. More important, Catholic Pentecostals exhibit a strong desire to legitimate their practices to fellow Catholics. They try hard to show their direct connection to the Catholic tradition and are aware that even the mere appearance of any unorthodoxy can pose a threat to potential members. Thus, "there is considerable attention paid, in charismatic literature, to the Catholic orthodoxy of their movement and to possible unorthodox practices which should be avoided."[22] This legitimist desire for acceptance within a nonbiblically fundamentalist church, McGuire claims, routinizes the charisma. Especially instructive is the tendency in Catholic charismatic circles to reduce prophesy to a merely affective (almost contentless) use, "because such prophesy is not likely to challenge the authority of the church hierarchy."[23] Moreover, leadership roles in Catholic prayer groups—in contradistinction to the Protestant Pentecostal practice—are widely shared and rotated, thus avoiding possible clashes between a powerful charismatic prayer leader and the hierarchy. By charting the evolution of a number of Catholic charismatic groups over a decade, McGuire details how, over time, the Catholic charismatic movement became less fundamentalist, more symbolic, and multifaceted in its understandings of Scripture and church authority.

McGuire's research should not surprise us since, as I contend, biblical fundamentalism has never been and is unlikely to become a characteristically Catholic form of fundamentalism. The rich resources of the institutional church are poised to ward off the danger of this form of fundamentalism. Rather, alluding to The Wanderer, The Remnant, and other Catholic right-wing integralist groups in the United States, San Francisco's Archbishop John R. Quinn warned of the dangers of a new integralism. What is Catholic integralism?

What constitutes its classic religious and social agenda? How does it compare and contrast with Protestant fundamentalism? How important is it to understand contemporary Catholicism?

Classic Catholic Integralism

In the last decades of the nineteenth century Catholicism, like Protestantism, had to come to grips with modernity in the forms of: higher-biblical criticism; the scientific, especially Darwinian, revolution; and the new forces of liberal, bourgeois democracy in Europe with its decided anticlerical stamp and its program of separation of church and state and social progress. Especially after the loss of the Papal States in 1870, European Catholicism felt under siege. Long allied in France with an antirevolutionary monarchist party, the church remained rooted in traditionalist politics. At Vatican I, in defiance of its loss of temporal power, the church escalated its spiritual claims by proclaiming the doctrine of papal infallibility.

Around the turn of the century, a number of Catholic scholars, notably Alfred Loisy in France and George Tyrell and Baron Friedrich von Hügel in England, sought a new Catholic rapprochement with modernity. They combined doctrinal with social modernism, much as liberal Protestantism, at the time, conjoined the social gospel with a project of dialogue—in Schliermacher's classic terms, "with the cultural despisers of religion."

The modernist movement in Catholicism was a loose, spontaneous movement of scholars in a number of countries, including the United States. None saw themselves as heretics. A very loose connection also existed between the modernist scholars and socially progressive movements open to the ideas of the French Republic (e.g., Marc Sangnier and the Le Sillon movement in France, Romolu Murri's movement for a Catholic socialism in Italy). Generally, the modernists saw their task as, in Loisy's terms, building a "true Catholicism of the future" and constructing a new Catholic apologetic based on the role of religion rather than by appealing to scholastic theology. They distanced themselves from many elements of Protestant higher criticism. Thus, in treating of Adolph von Harnack's discussion of the essence of Christianity, Loisy insisted that: (1) it is not possible to separate the Christian idea from the Christian community (and, hence, from historic Catholicism); and (2) it is not possible to isolate any one feature of Christianity as the invariable essence of the Bible. Despite Loisy's attempts to differentiate his position from Harnack's and secular modernists, his thought, in Rome, was perceived as one with these Protestant and secular modernists.

A group of Roman curial insiders, executing a coup of "bureaucratic insurgency," saw in the incipient and unorganized efforts of these scholars (whose sympathizers may have numbered, at the movement's high point, barely 1,500) an alleged international conspiracy against the papacy and Catholicism.[24] In fact, the so-called conspiracy consisted of nothing more than letters and travels of von Hügel. But, "the ecclesiastical elites recognized and capitalized on the possibility of fortifying their own position by constructing a caricature of the modernists' position through weaving their opponents' views into a coherent whole and condemning modernism as a heresy.[25] The Catholic modernists were unfairly lumped together with secular anticlerical and Masonic enemies of the church. Indeed, they were perceived as more dangerous than these external enemies. For, "dissidents working in an organization are within its networks and authority structure and hence are more likely to attract followers than are external critics who can make no legitimate claims."[26]

Writing about such scapegoating of "deviant insiders," sociologist Lewis Coser notes, "the search for or invention of a dissenter within may serve to maintain a structure which is threatened from outside."[27] In 1907 Pope Pius X condemned modernism in the church as the synthesis of all heresies, and the full force of the Roman hierarchy was marshalled to crush it. Five of Loisy's books were placed on the Index of Forbidden Books, and both Loisy and Tyrell were excommunicated. Numerous scholars were removed from their teaching posts, and an antimodernist oath was required of all priests (yearly renewed by seminary professors until the 1960s). A secret international organization (the Sapinière) and diocesan "vigilance committees" were set up to detect and report any signs of the modernist heresy in the church. Countless clerics were harassed, censured, relieved of their posts, and stripped of their credentials. Thus, a veritable reign of terror against the world of scholarship ensued. By 1920 church modernists had been crushed or, at least, forced deeply underground.

Several similarities between Catholic integralism and Protestant fundamentalism deserve noting:

1. Chronologically, both occurred during the first and second decades of the twentieth century when the forces of a new synthesis between liberalism and religion began to make inroads in both Catholicism and Protestantism.

2. Both movements represent a synthesis of a theological position and an ideological-political stance against the erosion of traditional authorities. Both are *antimoderne* and literalist. In Protestantism, the authority under attack was the infallible inerrancy of Scripture; in Catholicism, it was the infallible inerrancy of papal authority. It deserves noting that the central symbols evoked by fundamentalist reaction (*sola scriptura* and papal primacy) remain central to larger Protestant and Catholic orthodoxy. The fundamentalists took central orthodox symbols and blew them out of proportion to form a caricature. But, by appealing to central symbols of orthodoxy, they could dip into larger constituencies and sensibilities within mainline Protestantism and Catholicism. They had potential allies in the mainstream. Daniel Alexander notes:

> When we compare integralism and fundamentalism, we are struck by the fact that both these currents appeal to the concept of infallibility (papal infallibility adopted at Vatican I for the former and the Bible's infallibility as expressed in the dogma of literal inspiration and of inerrancy, asserted at more or less the same time, for the latter). In both cases, we have been led to see in this appeal a defense of the objectivity of the structure of religious tradition threatened by the rise of liberal subjectivism and by the shattering of religious meanings as a result of secularization.[28]

3. In both cases, the debate between fundamentalists and liberals (in Protestantism) and modernists and integralists (in Catholicism) is caught up in a polemical field of discourse. The terms used to describe the parties in dispute are not value-neutral. Thus, "in Catholic milieux the word 'integrism' was first used by opponents of those who called themselves 'Integral Catholics,' just as the word 'modernism' was immediately used by the Roman hierarchy to disqualify the

scholars."[29] Daniel Alexander speaks to this point. In both cases (e.g., Protestant fundamentalism and Catholic integralism), "it is clear that right from the start the concept escapes an unambiguous social identification process as it is invested with the meaning given it by its opponents. The sociologist must, therefore, take into account the whole polemic field to which it belongs."[30] We do not have polemic-free, value-neutral terms for liberal Protestants, fundamentalists, integralists, and Catholic modernists.

4. Neither the integralists nor fundamentalists are *antimoderne* in every respect. Both groups are notorious for their willingness to adapt the latest organizational structures and technological devises to spread their message (the fundamentalists turn to the electronic church). Nor are they always naive or uncritical about the currents of modernity. French sociologist Alaine Touraine notes of reactionary social movements that their "fundamental aim contains an organized attempt on the part of some agents to control the historicity of a specific community."[31] Unlike withdrawing and world-rejecting sects, fundamentalist antimodernists seek to be *in* modernity (and to influence its direction) but not to be *of* it.

Alexander registers what was really at issue between the modernists and integralists:

> It is not the battle between tradition and modernity, but rather a divergence in their assessment of the means the church must resort to in order to reconquer modernity. Modernists think the church must adapt itself to the republican and secular definition of public space and Catholic exegesis must embrace the presuppositions of "scientific criticism" in order to remain credible in its new situation. Integralists, like Benigni, believe it is possible for the church to be present in its time precisely because it remains aware that it alone has social legitimacy because it is always deeply rooted in society. For modernists, it is possible to get involved in the political game as it is, for integralists, intransigence demands precisely that one acts and that one appears as a church and for the church; there is no need for Catholicism to become democratic. It is rather the Christian Democracy which should become Catholic. The integralists, thus, feel that there is not a bipolar opposition between good conservatives and modernist extremists, but rather a tripartite structure: on the right are those who turn their backs on their own era whom they call traditionalists; on the extreme left are those who are ready to sacrifice everything to modernity whom they call the modernists because they

misunderstand their own era. In between the two, integralists find the correct balance.[32]

Thus, neither fundamentalists nor integralists typically see themselves as *antimoderne*. Nor do they see themselves as a group that rejects confrontation with its own time.

5. As social science scholars, we are mainly interested in the various fundamentalisms because of their cultural-political spin-offs and political programs. Early on, for example, the integralist program became closely linked to the antirevolutionary, paleofascist politics of the *Action Française* in France.[33] Such intransigence of the integralists is caught in the remarks of Georges Goyau in the 1898 *Congres de l'Association de la Jeunesse Française,* where Goyau called for a great refusal of the inevitability of modernity, "a refusal which expresses a will to shape the world in a way which is different from that of non-Christian forces."[34] It is this active will to shape a different world that distinguishes fundamentalism from traditionalism.

Alaine Touraine notes that it is precisely because these antimodernist movements are determined by the opposition they oppose and arouse—and because they organize themselves insofar as they can label their opponents—"that they are open to other conflicts in society as a whole and help to stir them up by crystallizing around two competing views of the world and two antagonistic ways of achieving a better society. This is why they are often a vehicle for the specific social protest of a group which is oppressed or in decline."[35]

The path followed by Msgr. Benigni, the animator of integralism, shows how integralism is basically a reactionary movement facing the crisis of legitimacy which Roman Catholicism confronted during the nineteenth century. The first enemy of integralists was liberalism and, in particular, its representatives in the church who described themselves as liberal Catholics which, in the eyes of the integralists, seemed a contradiction in terms. Both Protestant fundamentalists and integralists trained their first artillery on these enemies within, and both focused first on the seminary and church journals as the key battleground for a new orthodoxy.

Like Charles Coughlin, the integralist American radio priest in the 1930s, Benigni claimed to embody in his movement "the social question," enunciated by Leo XIII in the encyclical, *Rerum Novarum*. However, despite the many contradictions inherent in the authoritarian populism typical of early integralism (something integralism shares with early Protestant fundamentalists such as William Jennings Bryan), the Catholic integralist groups in Europe shared an affinity with fascism. In the end, Benigni supported Mussolini, not because the latter really satisfied him but "because the rise of fascism, by making a clean sweep of a political system into which the church did not fit, speeded up, in Benigni's eyes, the possibility of setting up a real party of Christian order which would usher in the final redemption of society."[36]

In a similar way, Catholic integralist thinkers lent ideological support to the protofascist regimes of Getulio Vargas in Brazil, Juan Perón in Argentina, Franco in Spain, Marshal Pétain in France, and Salazar in Portugal. In this century, Catholic integralist movements harbor anti-Semitism and support militaristic solutions. In the postwar period they have championed the cold war ideology or, in Latin America, the national security ideology. In some cases the national security ideology in Latin America explicitly draws on the writings of Catholic integralist thinkers of the 1920s and 1930s.[37] By superimposing a political dimension on its conflicts with modernity, both integralism and fundamentalism mobilize around symbols of nationalist patriotism.

Differences between Fundamentalism and Integralism

If there are important similarities between Protestant fundamentalism and Catholic integralism, there are also essential differences:

1. The political program of integralism is always mediated in and through the church. For Benigni, as Emile Poulat notes, "in both senses of the word, the Catholic cannot but get lost in the world unless he lives in it as part of the church."[38] Protestant fundamentalists, however, possess a much stronger individualist and voluntaristic mediation for action, which allows transdenominational alliances and social movements. Due to its nature, Protestant fundamentalism can take on very different forms and owes less than meets the eye to any given era, since its ability to catalyze a return to

Christian civilization depends more on an additive set of individual moral decisions than on a political triumph of the corporate church as such. Whereas the ecclesiology of integralists does not accept democratic voluntarism, that of the fundamentalists does.

Integralists are constrained by their orthodoxy to be papal legitimists. Hence, as occurred in the period after World War II, if papal policy moves away from integralism toward greater accommodation with modernity—for example, toward adapting a Christian Democratic strategy in the political order, toward openness to scholarship in the biblical, patristic, and liturgical renewal movements—integralists are constrained by their legitimist orthodoxy, at least on the surface, to go along. The Vatican has often used and cast aside integralist movements to suit its own purposes. As the excommunication of Archbishop Marcel Lefebvre demonstrates, papal condemnation of integralist groups may lead to widespread defections from the group back to Rome. Integralism ceased to be a serious Catholic issue after 1940, until its recent world wide resurgence in the post-Vatican church.

2. In the end, the mainline Protestant response to Henry Emerson Fosdick's landmark sermon in 1922, "Shall the Fundamentalists Win?", led them to hold the line against the fundamentalists within their midst. These latter seceded to found their own seminaries, churches, journals, mission organizations, indeed, their own enclosed social world. In Catholic terms, they went into schism. Protestant fundamentalism lost its battle to control the bureaucracies of mainline Protestantism. The Catholic case of fundamentalism, however, involved a strategic alliance between Vatican bureaucrats and dissident social movements within the church (such as *Action Française*). When the institutional church accepted nonfundamentalist teachings of the relation of tradition to modernity—after Pius XI (who condemned *Action Française*) and Pius XII (who encouraged modern biblical scholarship) and, especially, after Vatican II—the surviving integralist groups were constrained, as papal legitimists, to go along. In a sometimes tortured rhetoric, contemporary Catholic integralist groups generally claim that they represent the authentic spirit and letter of Vatican II.[39] As long as the Vatican's curial bureaucrats are not pure integralists, it is difficult for the movements to

be so, short of schism. The cognitive dissonance exercised on papal fundamentalists by the notion of schism from the papacy generally suffices to keep them in the fold, on a papal leash.

3. Protestant fundamentalism's political energies are filtered through a potent millenarian imagination based on dispensationalist readings of the *Book of Revelation* and chiliastic expectations of the rapture. Catholic integralists rarely speak of the Second Coming of Christ or cataclysmic transitions to Christ's kingdom. Their main political complaint suggests, rather, that modernity and secularization have gone quite far enough. It is now time for "the true Catholics" to take a stand before things get even worse. Perhaps millenarianism is not an essential trait of fundamentalist reactions to modernity.

To the extent that a millenarian imagination is found within Catholic integralist groups, it is more likely to be linked to Marian symbolism, as Victor and Edith Turner note.[40] While these versions of modern Marian devotion (based on "secrets," on picturing the Madonna as the Virgin of the Apocalypse, and on tying Marian devotion to the Cold War) are often found within Catholic integralist groups, they are neither exclusive to them nor definitive of their general stance. Marian millenarianism, then, has very little direct political content (except a general skewing toward anticommunist and morally conservative parties).

Lester Kurtz has argued that, ironically, it was the Vatican's posture of heresy-hunting in the early twentieth century that elicited a reform movement among scholars who might otherwise never have created one. First cautiously, then more openly, the modernist scholars transformed the church. If in 1920 the modernist movement was dead, by the 1960s and 1970s, in the wake of Vatican Council II, the modernist program had been adopted by the official church.[41]

Contemporary Integralism

Is Catholic integralism really dead, then, in the post-Vatican church? On the contrary, a resurgent integralism can be found throughout the world church. In Europe, the principal integralist movements include Archbishop Marcel Lefebvre's Fraternity of St. Pius X (strong in

France and Switzerland and closely allied in France with the national populist movement of Jean Le Pen), the Spanish foundation Opus Dei, and the Italian-based Communion and Liberation. It was these integralist movements which the bishops had in mind in the 1987 Synod of Bishops when they feared the free hand of "movements" in the church.

Lefebvre, like earlier integralists, opposes the false values of the French Revolution, which he sees now infecting the church: "*Liberté* was embodied in the pernicious doctrine of religious freedom; *egalité* was expressed in 'collegiality,' the idea that all the bishops of the world formed a team with the pope, thus undermining the papal monarchy; while *fraternité* took the form of ecumenism which allegedly masked the differences between Christians."[42] Lefebvre sees his movement as a "faithful remnant" and believes there has been no legitimate pope since the death of Pius XII in 1958.

Opus Dei (which is also very influential in Peru and other Latin American settings) provided the Franco governments with several cabinet ministers. Communion and Liberation (which sponsors its own Italian political party against the "secularization" of the Christian Democratic Party) sees itself also as a kind of savior of the church and restorer of authentic Catholic values. Giuseppe Lazatti, former rector of the Catholic University of Milan and a close ally of Pope Paul VI, comments on Communion and Liberation: "They define themselves as the one true church, and the only valid Christianity is their kind. At the start they would not even go to mass with anyone else. I don't see how it is possible to come to an understanding with them."[43] Elsewhere in Europe, the Confrontatie group in Holland has revived the heresy-hunting of the Sapinière group, constituting itself a "vigilance committee" in the Dutch church and lending support to the newly founded orthodox Roman Catholic Party.[44]

In Latin America, the principal integralist movement (besides Opus Dei) is Tradition, Family, Property, which has supported the dictatorships in Brazil and Chile.[45] In the United States, the principal integralist groups are Catholics United for the Faith, the True Catholics, the Remnant, and the Wanderer Forum. These groups represent a throwback to earlier Catholic fundamentalist hopes for a creeping infallibility to cover all areas of life. These various national groups are highly influential in Vatican circles and engage in extensive correspondence about sermons heard, theologians read, and catechism classes observed.

I recently performed a content analysis of two Catholic integralist journals, *The Wanderer* and *The Remnant*. According to both journals, whose rhetoric is explicitly religious, the principal enemy lies within the church—those who have sold out to modernity. Yet, despite disclaimers of being in any way political, *The Wanderer* and *The Remnant* include a political program. With Protestant fundamentalists, these neointegralist journals believe a dominant "secular humanism" pervades American culture. Articles in *The Wanderer* strongly support an ideological anticommunism of the Cold War era (with many explicit appeals of support for the Contras). *The Wanderer* opposes government spending on welfare and suggests that racism is an overblown theme in American society. Politically, *The Wanderer* is strongly promarket and proconservative.

Nor is *The Wanderer* totally against resorting to domestic violence. One *Wanderer* article praises two men who, "in the space of fifteen minutes on Christmas eve, 1984, managed to give three priceless birthday presents to Jesus." These men are now serving sentences in a Tallahassee, Florida, prison for bombing abortion facilities. Another *Wanderer* article notes, "The Communists more and more openly treat a Democratic Party victory as a virtual victory for communism." The political sympathies of articles in *The Remnant* look quite similar. Yet, remarkably, neointegralists deny that integralism has any political views or program.[46]

Conclusions

1. The importance of the earlier integralist-modernist controversies rests on the fact that this 80-year-old controversy set a tone for dealing with a perennial Catholic issue that still haunts contemporary Catholicism. As Kurtz states, "The issue of modernism was fundamentally a conflict between ecclesiastical authority and the authority of independent scholars."[47] At the turn of the century, the conflict turned on explicitly dogmatic definitions and issues. Today

the focus has shifted to moral, especially sexual, issues. The condemnation of Charles Curran, Leonardo Boff, and Hans Küng suggests that the modernist-integralist controversy in contemporary Catholicism is not over yet.

2. Although few in number and sociologically unrepresentative of mainline Catholicism (including the majority of the episcopacy), the neointegralist groups enjoy disproportionate power in the Vatican curia. In the 1970s, Confrontatie in the Netherlands specialized in denouncing erring theologians and catechists. On most issues, their journal was the best predictor of Vatican curial actions against the bishops. In time, the Dutch episcopacy has become paralyzed and Confrontatie has acquired bishops to their liking. In the 1980s Catholics United for the Faith and the Wanderer Forum have stalked American theologians and even archbishops such as Seattle's Raymond Hunthausen and Milwaukee's Rembert Weakland. While their complaints against Hunthausen and Weakland are mainly couched in legalistic and liturgical terms, in both cases the archbishops represent notable episcopal voices for a politics of disarmament and economic justice. Moreover, as earlier in the Netherlands, preoccupation with the pesky and persistent integralist attacks are likely to considerably lessen episcopal inclinations to pursue a forthright social agenda.

3. As noted in Europe and Latin America, integralist groups share an analysis of modernity counter to that of Vatican II's decree, *The Church in the Modern World*. As with classical integralism, their religious agenda often masks both a triumphal reassertion of the church as "a perfect society" and strategic alliances with conservative reactionary political movements.

In the final analysis, however, a polemic view of fundamentalism might overlook ways in which such groups are often shrewder in their diagnosis of the dangers of modernity than in the heteronomous authoritarian responses they espouse. Gabriel Daly picks up on this point, on which I will end this essay:

> The existence of a fundamentalist movement in all historical faiths is a phenomenon which should neither surprise nor disturb the reflective believer. It is, in part at least, a protest against the intimations of lost in-

nocence. . . . From Tertullian on, there has always been some degree of protest in Christianity about what intellectuals are alleged to do to the purity and strength of faith. Not all of this protest can be simply dismissed as irrationalism. It poses an important question, at least for church-affiliated theologians. How is it that when religious belief and practice are brought in harmony with reasonable requirements of the secular world, so often they lose their power to attract and to satisfy? It sometimes seems that a church which squares up with modernity loses precisely the "Dionysian" element which fundamentalism so often preserves. . . . The Kantian ideal of "religion within the limits of reason" is, in the end, the most unreasonable aim of all, because it neglects an element in human nature which is both necessary to spiritual health and impervious to the censorship of reason. Popular religion, even in its most superstitious, anti-intellectual, or emotionalist manifestations may be telling us something we do not want to hear in academe. Just as the cigarette manufacturers are compelled to display a warning on the cigarette package, so perhaps faculties and departments of theology might be profitably compelled to display in their lecture halls the warning, "Dionysus always strikes back"—which is only another way of expressing the New Testament conviction that the Spirit breathes where he wills.[48]

Notes

1. See Jürgen Habermas, *The Theory of Communicative Action* (Boston: Beacon Press, 1984).

2. See Edward Shils, *Tradition* (Chicago: University of Chicago Press, 1981).

3. For some distinctions among fundamentalism, conservatism, and traditionalism, see a special issue of *Lumiere et Vie*, especially the article by Pierre La Thuiliere, "Le Fondamentalisme dans les Traditions Chretiennes," pp. 69–85.

4. Lester Kurtz, *The Politics of Heresy* (Berkeley: University of California Press, 1986).

5. Daniel Alexander, "Is Fundamentalism an Integrism?" *Social Compass* 32, no. 4 (1985): 373–92.

6. *A Pastoral Statement for Catholics on Biblical Fundamentalism* (Washington, D.C.: National Conference of Catholic Bishops, 1987).

7. Gabriel Daly, "Catholicism and Modernity," *Journal of the American Academy of Religion* 53, no. 3 (December 1985): 794.

8. I do not agree with James Davidson Hunter's equation of fundamentalism with orthodoxy in his *American Evangelicalism: Conservatism, Reli-*

gion and the Quandary of Modernity (New Brunswick, N.J.: Rutgers University Press, 1983).

9. Kurtz, Politics of Heresy, p. 15.

10. Besides Kurtz, several other good accounts of the modernist vs. integralist controversy are: Maude Petre, Von Hügel and Tyrell: The Story of a Friendship (New York: Dutton, 1937); Alfred Loisy: His Significance (Cambridge: Cambridge University Press, 1944); Emile Poulat, Integrisme et Catholicisme Integral (Paris: Casterman, 1969).

11. Cited in Kurtz, Politics of Heresy, p. 1.

12. These scurrilous pamphlets are available from Chick Publications, P.O. Box 662, Chino, Calif; for Maria Monk and anti-Catholicism as a theme in America, see Barbara Welter, "From Maria Monk to Paul Blanschard: A Century of Protestant Anti-Catholicism," in Robert Bellah and Frederick Greenspahn, eds., Uncivil Religion: Interreligious Hostility in America (New York: Crossroad, 1987), pp. 43–72.

13. Personal communication from Karl Keating. See his "Answering the Fundamentalist Challenge," Homiletic and Pastoral Review 85, no. 10 (July 1985): 32, 52–57.

14. See George Gallup and Jim Castelli, The American Catholic People (Garden City, N.Y.: Doubleday, 1987), p. 139.

15. Dean Kelley, Why the Conservative Churches are Growing (New York: Harper and Row, 1972).

16. Karl Keating, Catholics and Fundamentalism (San Francisco: Ignatius Press, 1988).

17. See Ann Carey, "Catholic College Students Lured by Fundamentalists," Our Sunday Visitor 75, no. 50 (April 12, 1987): 3–4.

18. John F. Whealon, "Challenging Fundamentalism," America 155, no. 7 (September 27, 1986): 136.

19. George Gallup, Princeton Religious Research Center, Emerging Trends 2, no. 1 (January 1980): 1.

20. Joseph Fichter, The Catholic Cult of the Paraclete (New York: Sheed and Ward, 1975), pp. 39–57.

21. Meredith McGuire, Pentecostal Catholics (Philadelphia: Temple University Press, 1982).

22. Ibid., p. 189.

23. Ibid., p. 103.

24. For the notion of bureaucratic insurgency, see Mayer N. Zald and Michael Berger, "Social Movements in Organizations, Coup d'Etat, Insurgency and Mass Movements," American Journal of Sociology 83 (January 1978): 823–61.

25. Kurtz, Politics of Heresy, p. 55.

26. Ibid., p. 12.

27. Lewis Coser, *The Functions of Social Conflict* (Glencoe, Ill.: The Free Press, 1956), p. 110.

28. Alexander, "Is Fundamentalism an Integrism?", p. 386.

29. Ibid., p. 374.

30. Ibid., p. 375.

31. Alaine Touraine, *La Voix et la Regard* (Paris: Editions Seuil, 1978), p. 104.

32. Alexander, "Is Fundamentalism an Integrism?", pp. 379–80.

33. For the *Action Française,* see Eugene Weber, *Action Française: Royalism and Reaction in Twentieth-Century France* (Stanford: Stanford University Press, 1962).

34. Cited in Emile Poulat, *Catholicisme, Democratie et Socialisme* (Tournai, Belgium: Casterman, 1977), p. 194.

35. Touraine, *La Voix et Le Regard*, p. 362.

36. Alexander, "Is Fundamentalism an Integrism?", p. 380.

37. For classic Catholic integralism during the regime of Getulio Vargas in Brazil, see Scott Mainwaring, *The Catholic Church and Politics in Brazil* (Stanford: Stanford University Press, 1986), pp. 30–34. For Catholic integralist contributions to the doctrine of the national security state ideology, see Joseph Comblin, *The Church and the National Security State* (Maryknoll, N.Y.: Orbis Press, 1979).

38. Poulat, *Catholicisme, Democratie et Socialisme*, p. 306.

39. For the often tortuous rhetoric of an integralist group, Catholics United for the Faith, claiming to act in the spirit of Vatican II, see Timothy Iglesias, "CUF and Dissent: A Case Study of Religious Conservatism," *America* 156, no. 14 (April 11, 1987): 303–7.

40. See Victor Turner and Edith Turner, *Image and Pilgrimage in Christian Culture* (New York: Columbia University Press, 1978), p. 171.

41. Kurtz, *Politics of Heresy*, pp. 181–83.

42. Peter Hebblethwaite, "A Roman Catholic Fundamentalism," *Times Literary Supplement* (August 5–11, 1988): 866.

43. Ibid., p. 866.

44. For *Opus Dei* as an integralist group, see Peter Hertel, "International Christian Democracy," in Gregory Baum and John A. Coleman, eds., *The Church and Christian Democracy* (Edinburgh: T. and T. Clark, 1987).

45. For a treatment of Tradition, Family, and Property, see Mainwaring, *The Catholic Church and Politics in Brazil*, pp. 70, 171. The classic treatment can be found in Charles Antoine, *O. Integrisme Brasiliero* (Rio de Janeiro: Editiones Voz, 1980).

46. Personal communication to me from the publisher of the *Wanderer.*

47. Kurtz, *Politics of Heresy,* p. 12.

48. Daly, "Catholicism and Modernity," pp. 795–96.

5

The Islamic Resurgence: Civil Society Strikes Back

EMMANUEL SIVAN

I

In the Middle East and North Africa, the 1950s and 1960s witnessed the highwater mark of the mass-mobilizing state, all-pervasive bureaucracy, mass production factory system, and official culture. This was the pinnacle of an evolution begun in the 1820s and greatly catalyzed since the decolonization. The gist of that process consisted in redrawing the age-old boundaries between state and civil society, with the former—which until the early nineteenth century had largely been a "watchdog state"—invading domains hitherto deemed the game reserve of voluntary associations and institutions: education, welfare, economic activity (especially production), popular culture, even family life.

What made the state's assault upon the already shrinking boundaries of civil society so effective and devastating was a combination of factors:

1. The new nationalist state was characterized by sincere and combative anti-imperialism, and hence could not be impugned as "collaborationist" and openly "westoxicated" as the old upper-class rulers used to be.

2. The elite of the new state was plebeian in origin and thus able to

address the masses in their own idiom. It was, furthermore, the carrier of a new and galvanizing indigenous ideology, Pan-Arabism, capable of attaining cultural hegemony and developing into a sort of secular religion with its own symbols, rituals, calendar (Gregorian rather than Islamic)—all in all, shaping man's notions of time and place, basic values, and everyday behavior.

3. The new ruling class was usually military in profession with all that this implies in terms of relative efficiency, cult of order, and penchant for ruthlessness and for disrespect of legality. It had at its service new population-control techniques learnt from like-minded European regimes of the right and of the left (as evidenced in the reorganization of the secret police, introduction of listening and other intelligence devices, detention camps, etc.). Repression could now be all-pervasive.

4. Last but not least, the technological revolution in audio-visual communications (notably the transistor radio and television), which coincided with the advent of the nationalist state, tended to favor the blatantly interventionist ambitions of the new masters. Assuring themselves of a virtual monopoly on the press and book publishing (supplemented by an ever-vigilant censorship vis-à-vis those media organs still held in private hands), these rulers perceived immediately the brainwashing potential of the new audio-visual media. These media could penetrate every nook and cranny, reaching the illiterate majority of the population—mainly women, small children, and rural residents—those hitherto outside the scope of the educational system (and, it goes without saying, of the printed media) due to their virtual seclusion from the public place, and/or their geographical distance. Thus privacy and periphery became less meaningful ramparts for civil society, not only with regard to repression but also to persuasion, all the more so as the fare that the new media were to sell was attractive in substance and in packaging: the nationalist gospel as focus of solidarity (deftly couched in Islamic terms hiding its secularized subtext) on the one hand; a consumerist ethos—economic, state-controlled modernization as the avenue for the good material life—on the other.

How pervasive is the state's influence on civil society? This cannot yet be established with a reasonable degree of precision. And although I am still in the process of reviewing the evidence (surveys, press reports, memoirs, short stories), it is quite possible that some of the success was more apparent than real; that many of the alarmist reports coming from fundamentalist circles with regard to the subjugation of religion and cultural activity suffer from excessive use of hyperbole. What *is* evident is that in certain areas the state encountered powerful resistance to its expansion. The best example is family planning, where the muted lack of collaboration on the part of medium- and lower-level *ulama*, coupled with solidly anchored values shared by rural and petite bourgeoisie populations, stymied any attempt to influence social mores in this, the most intimate zone of human life (the major exception, and not an enduring one, is Tunisia). In other fields as well the state may be less powerful than its rhetoric would indicate. For instance, if for no other reason than sheer lack of funds, the nation-states did not embark upon a serious program of kindergarten and prekindergarten schooling. Thus, socialization was still largely a matter of the (usually extended) family, though that "ever-present baby sitter," television, began to play a substantial role.

Nevertheless, it is undeniable that the state's assault on civil society was largely successful. I agree with Leonard Binder that a crucial test in this type of inquiry is what happens to formal and semiformal institutions (as distinct from associations). Here the victory of the new authoritarian state is impressive: parliaments were coerced into a rubber-stamp mentality; political parties were outlawed and those that went underground were effectively persecuted; trade unions were disbanded or forced to merge into a state-controlled unitary organization; the press (especially daily and weekly) was nationalized or subject to stringent controls; book publishing and book imports were transformed into a state monopoly (whether directly by law or through efficient use of censorship). Religious institutions did not escape the interventionistic state: *shari'a* courts were either abolished and forced to merge with the civil courts system or were placed under its aegis and control; *waqf* endowments were tightly supervised; ulama training was integrated into the state educational system; and the ulama in their rostrums were used as propagandists for the regime. Last, but certainly not least, the hitherto largely independent civil judiciary was cowed into servile obedience (with recalcitrants summarily fired and replaced by docile new appointees); and wherever particularly "dirty" or problematic tasks existed, military courts (often dubbed "state security courts")—their realm greatly expanded—could be relied upon to perform them.

There were obviously differences in degree and scope among the various modernized countries: in Iran, for instance, the ulama domain proved to be quite impregnable; in Jordan and Morocco the state court system had to resign itself to coexist with the custom lay system. And there were likewise variations in the curtailment of ethnic or regional autonomous institutions. The direction of the development of these states is, however, more or less the same.

Similar is the persistent attempt of all of these states to create a set of brand new institutions (unitary party, youth and women's movements, intellectuals' associations)—presumably voluntary but under effective state control—designed to mobilize the population and, perhaps more important, to assure the state of a "presence" (in Gramsci's sense of the term) in all walks of life. Coupled with the institution-building was the creation of a national civil religion (already alluded to) with its panoply of heroes, symbols, sacred places (monuments, historical sites), sacred times (holidays, memorial days), and above all, myths. These could be "founding myths," relating to the nation's or the regime's origins, or future-oriented—sort of eschatological—myths referring to their goals and aspirations. The enactment of these myths was mostly in the public place and anchored in the here and now, as evidenced in ceremonies, for example. Their success in shaping not only behavior but also basic attitudes to primordial (and intensely private) issues such as sex and gender, death and the hereafter, is debatable—as proven by, among others, the studies of Imad al-Din Sultan (1972) on the Egyptian middle class, and of Sayyid Uways (1971) and Manufi (1980) on Egypt's peasants and the urban lower classes. But in most areas of social behavior, cultural hegemony was no doubt appropriated by the new rulers, all the more aggressively as time wore on due to the technological advances in the field of electronic media.

2

Buttressed by the state's expanding economic role—notably in dol-
ing out public sector and civil service jobs for school graduates, and
in shrinking, through nationalization, the economic basis of the
middle-class autonomy, i.e., the crux of the old civil society—the
new hegemony appeared impregnable from 1960 to 1965. Although
the tide was soon reversed and civil society began to expand, this
reversal actually confirms the above evaluation of the state's dyna-
mism, persistent initiative, and relative success. For the reversal was
based not in civil society's vigor and initiative but rather in the state's
failures. These failures mean that in certain domains the state was
unable to modify its people's core values in relation to the ultimate
meaning of life. Even more important, the dramatic reverses and
debacles the state suffered during the 1960s brought into question
not only its claim to represent an inevitable historical tide but also
the feasibility (and justification) of many of its goals. As a result, both
those committed to its cause and those who had joined not out of
conviction but through sheer opportunism became a less recurrent
phenomenon. The list of these debacles is long and well known, so
suffice it to mention the most obvious: the breakup of the UAR and
the Yemen War as the first heavy blows to Pan-Arabism; the 1967
war, which hit the credibility of the military elites; the economic
recession of 1965–67, which punctured the myth of public sector
dominance as the panacea to rapid GNP growth and to the instant
gratification of spiraling material expectations.

Only when the state was sorely weakened did the Islamic resurgence begin to challenge the newly established borders between
state and civil society. True, like any such social phenomenon, the
resurgence had its precursors—Sayyid Qutb in Egypt, Khomeini in
Iran—who had developed a set of core ideas (related, among others, to
the state-society relationship) by the time the state had reached its
zenith of power. But theirs were lonely voices in the desert, and social
receptivity was virtually nonexistent. It took the debacles—in Iran's
case, the state's unsuccessful attempts in the early 1970s to fulfill
rising expectations and to limit the damage of social dislocations
created by rapid modernization—in order for these ideas to gain a

sizable number of adherents. Khomeini is a rare case of a "precursor" who lived to become a "pioneer" (in Mannheim's terms) and to lead a movement anchored in the very ideas he had put forward. He owed his success to the shah's relative leniency and to his own longevity. Sayyid Qutb's fate was much more in line with the historical precedents studied by Mannheim. It was given to other, much younger people to pioneer the resurgence for which he had laid the foundation.

The Islamic resurgence can be explained to a large extent by the durability of the Islamic "traditional bedrock," i.e., the persistence—through constant adaptation—of classical Islam as a *living tradition*, especially with regard to basic attitudes toward the fundamentals of human existence. However, this beleaguered bastion would not have recaptured the initiative had there not occurred the series of failures described above coupled with the subsequent failure of nerve and ebbing initiative on the part of the state's elites. This is a crucial point, for although the prospects of the resurgence would seem to depend on its actions, they are also inversely related to the state's performance. In other words, the worse the state's record in gratifying economic needs, in creating and transmitting a nation-state (and no more a suprastate) *mystique,* the better the chances of the resurgence. The paradox is—and this is a topic that requires more detailed empirical research—that some of the means employed by the rulers in the 1970s and 1980s (e.g., expansion of the public sector, greater political pluralism, broader autonomy of the judiciary) tend to buttress civil society, which forms the very basis of the fundamentalist tide.

3

Against this background, the Islamic resurgence may be interpreted as a response of civil society to the state's debacles, recapturing the initiative and redrawing the boundaries between the two. That this response took an Islamic character highlights the validity of Gramsci's thesis as to the vital importance of everyday culture. For if everyday culture is made of "various layers and deposits, infinite traces with no inventory," it is evident that even in the heyday of the new state, these deposits had one thing in common: they were for the most part Islamic. The survival of the *hijri* calendar, punctuating the rhythm of everyday life (alongside and above the state's Gregorian calendar of holidays and memorial days), the broader appeal and mass participation in religious ceremonies and festivities, are but the most obvious instances of this endurance, even as the religious tradition was battered by consumerism, mass recreation, and other deleterious innovations (*bid'a*).

It is thus understandable why the resurgence channeled so much of its energy into modifying the division of spheres between state and society. The participant-observer studies—carried, *inter alia,* by Kepel, Guenana, and the present writer in Egypt; by Fischer in Iran; by Seurat and Shapiro in Lebanon; by Waltz in Tunisia; and by Mayer in the Israeli-occupied Gaza strip—provide ample evidence of the primary importance of this strategy of reconquering civil society. The strategy was greatly facilitated by the fact that technological developments tended, at long last, to favor civil society autonomy rather than state control: cases in point are tape cassettes, Xeroxing, offset printing techniques, and most recently, videos. Though more research must be done on these issues, the strategies can be summarized as follows:

1. Reestablishment of a patchwork of voluntary associations (*jama'at*)—based upon age, gender, occupation, social position, or residence—arrogating to themselves above all educational and ritualistic functions, but sometimes also trade unionist ones (e.g., for students, shopkeepers, and craftsmen) and serving always as foci for sociability, particularly for uprooted strata (e.g., migrants from the countryside to town, or from provincial towns to a metropolis).

2. While jama'at-type groups take as their original basis of operations the hitherto uninvaded private domain (usually the home or the remaining *ahli* mosques), they move swiftly into the public place. A prime tactic in the service of this strategy is the creeping but persistent invasion of public mosques, either through conversion or "buying out" of their poorly paid personnel, so mistreated in the past by the state apparatus. In many cases the invasion or "recuperation" of the public mosque (often formerly an ahli one) is accomplished by intimidation.

3. The same mixture of persuasion and intimidation—modeled on the state's former "carrot and stick" tactics—is also found in the greater use of vigilante-style action (enforcing the fast on Ramadan, prohibiting one from watching licentious TV programs or listening to rock music, respecting the prohibition of alcoholic beverages, and imposing the injunctions on modest attire for women). The trend in recent years, as the movement grows more assertive, is toward a more frequent and daring use of violence (e.g., burning movie houses and video clubs) and toward the systematic expansion of space monopolized by the movement's ethos (segregated lecture halls, banning "blue" movies and video cassettes).

4. Where such concessions are difficult to get or too slow in coming, the associations—whose vitality and amoebic expansion is the best indicator of the renaissance of civil society—tend to fall back on self-help, creating their own autonomous social space. They fund gender-segregated shuttle buses for students; organize study groups and summer camps; found cooperatives and shops that have no recourse to interest-carrying loans (and which, of course, also provide employment for the fundamentalist clientele); and fund charitable associations which provide health care and social welfare predicated on Islamic norms (care segregated by gender, loans that are interest-free, etc.). In the last two or three years there have also been initiatives—mostly in Jordan and Egypt—in preschool education and in enrichment programs for school children, both domains in which the state had always been deficient.

5. A no less effective, but insufficiently documented line of action, relates to the creeping invasion (or "recapturing," if you will) of the judiciary. In Tunisia and Egypt there are a growing number of instances of judges—inspired and/or applauded by the fundamentalists—who rule according to the shari'a, especially in cases where state legislation is ambiguous, but also where the Islamic law runs counter to the state laws (i.e., on matters related to interest-based banking). Likewise there are a few reports on the growing popularity of "pacts" entered into by members of jama'at, according to which the signatories agree to bypass state courts (notably in civil litigation) and go instead to fundamentalist imams who serve as arbiters and rule exclusively by the shari'a.

It should be emphasized, however, that even where the movement is quite successful, as is the case in Egypt, a Muslim "counter-society" (to borrow P. Nettle's term) as foreshadowed by tactics (4) and (5) is still an ideal rather than a reality. For one thing, some of the more important ventures in this direction—such as Sheikh Hafiz Salamah's Abbasiyah complex in northern Cairo—encountered substantial financial and management difficulties. And for another, one should not underestimate the capacity of the beleaguered state to heap one obstacle after another upon the road of such ventures, e.g., through the shrewd use of licensing and zoning regulations and by putting counterpressures on recalcitrant judges. Which brings us once again to the finding noted above: that the continued expansion of civil society's sphere by the Islamic resurgence depends to a large extent on what the state will do—in the present context, what the state might do to contain the resurgence either by repressive means and "divide and rule" tactics (particularly effective vis-à-vis the decentralized Sunni resurgence) or by providing better social services. The irony once again, as with the expansion of the public sector, is that some of the "active defense" tactics employed by the state—i.e., a greater role for parliament, a measure of political pluralism and broader freedom of expression—might serve to buttress the Islamic resurgence, with its goal of creating an alternate and autonomous society. Eventually, such an alternate society, secure in its cultural hegemony, may even serve as a basis for the seizure of power, exactly in line with the Gramsci scenario. But even disregarding such an eventuality (which for the moment, one should admit, looks far-fetched), the mere fact that the state has recourse to the tactics outlined here contributes to the redrawing of the boundaries in favor of civil society.

4

Perhaps the most interesting paradox in a story replete with ironies and paradoxes relates to the future aspirations of the Islamic resurgence, as they can be extrapolated from various scenarios produced under the movement (and cross-checked against the postrevolutionary developments in Iran). As one reads such writings one perceives instantly that Islamic radicals aspire to establish a "contemporary state" (*hukuma 'asriyya*), one in tune with the twentieth century with regard to means and modalities, though not in values. The writings do hold as a sort of mythical reference to the seventh-century state of Muhammad and the early caliphs (all four orthodox caliphs, for the Sunnis, or 'Ali only for the Shiites). But this applies to broad moral principles and does not imply a return to a medieval form and method of government. Unlike the seventh-century state (or, for that matter, almost all premodern Muslim states), this is to be a strong and actively interventionist state, not one confined to foreign affairs, defense policy, and certain areas of commerce. The medieval Muslim watchdog state—which left civil society largely to its own devices—is gone forever. Technological changes, especially in transportation and communication, enabled the modern state in the Middle East to intervene in areas hitherto left to voluntary forms of association (and greatly influenced by men of religion). The upshot of it all, say the radicals, is that Islam was pushed to the sidelines in education, family mores, leisure, economic initiative, and so on. To counter this trend of de-Islamization, the radicals propose to take the modern state and use its own tools to Islamize society; there is no sense in dismantling this state or outlawing the technology it utilizes. Technology cannot be written off by juristic fiat; it can only be regulated. A case in point is television, which is subject to tight state control in order to shape hearts and minds. Likewise, whatever their economic predilections, the radicals are agreed on one point: there is no going back to the hands-off policy of the pre-nineteenth-century Middle Eastern states (or, for that matter, of the Prophet's state). This much is clear even from the debates between pragmatists and ideologues within the present Iranian political elite. The former wish to extend the private sector, but they remain dedicated to state control of key sectors (oil, military industry, heavy industry, etc.) and to a measure of state intervention in order to achieve redistribution of income and wealth.

The adaptation of past molds to present realities is to be made through the use of *ijtihad* (innovation in matters of jurisprudence) which all radicals endorse, provided it is kept in the hands of the "virtuous" (i.e., the radicals themselves) and not conferred upon just any Muslim learned in the law (as Islamic modernists would have it). The primacy of Muslim law (the shari'a)—which is crucial to the Islamic revolutionary myth—can thus be preserved while allowing the state to be contemporary and powerful.

In this state's agenda, matters pertaining to education, communication, and entertainment are going to loom large. This is where, according to radicals' diagnosis, "westoxication" had its most deleterious and rapid impact; hence, to counter it is the most urgent task. The state's nearly complete monopoly in these domains will give the revolutionaries the means to that end. A purge of the present media and the school system by the future Islamic state is thus a vital necessity. (In fact, these are the areas into which the Iranian regime moved first and in the swiftest manner.) The outlawing of "anti-Islamic" scientific theories by the state is to be expected, a measure not perceived to contradict the "contemporary state." The radicals are content to use technological applications of science, and do not care for the basic research most of them are predicated upon (particularly in fields like molecular biology, astrophysics, and geology, which inch too close for comfort to the essential verities of religion). They resign themselves to backwardness in science, hoping for an up-to-date transfer of technology from abroad. They are even ready to accept a certain lag if the transfer does not operate as smoothly as hoped; and, needless to say, they refuse technology that may create thorny ethical problems (e.g., genetic engineering). This underlying attitude toward the preeminence of the "satanic" West in the realm of technology is best exemplified in arms procurement and in medicine. It is emblematic that when gravely ill, the major proponent of Sunni radicalism, the Pakistani Mawlana Mawdoodi, went to the United States for treatment (where he was eventually to die). What holds for technology in the service of brainwashing or in defense against external enemies, also holds for surveillance and mass control techniques. It is likewise clear that in an Islamic state, the "westoxicated" will not be allowed the free use of tape cassettes and other reactive, feedback media technology which the fundamentalists now use to solidify their presence in civil society.

Which brings us to an even more crucial irony. However much they critique the "nondemocratic practices" of the present regimes, it is evident from their tracts that the Muslim radicals flatly reject democracy as being predicated on manmade laws, and thus contradicting the law system set by Allah, i.e., the shari'a. The attempts by modernists to show that Islam may be compatible with democracy are treated with cold disdain—as typical of the apologetic mode that accepts Western criteria and endeavors to make Islam conform to them. The reason is obvious: conformity with contemporary civilization in the domain of values is unacceptable a priori. The liquidation of basic democratic liberties in the name of the shari'a follows necessarily. And that entails a restriction of civil society's sphere (even compared with the present situation), particularly with regard to formal institutions.

Although some form of parliamentary representation may endure, it will take a back seat to revolutionary institutions. This is made amply clear in the "draft constitution" that the Islamic Republic of Lebanon prepared under Hizbolla aegis in 1985: in the absence of the Hidden Imam, the source of all authority is the Virtuous Jurist who will appoint the chairman of the Lebanese Governance of the Jurist Commission, a local ayatollah. The commission, made up of representatives of all religious communities, will be the ultimate locus of all legislative, judicial, and executive powers. Among others, it will oversee the election by universal suffrage of the president of the republic and of the Islamic Consultative (*shura*) Council, and will have the power to dissolve the council. Significantly, the word "democracy" does not appear in the draft. Sunni scenarios, while much less detailed, carry the same message.

The fundamentalists' greatest services to civil society are, consequently, rendered in opposition. But either in opposition or eventually in power, they never envision the dismantling or gross enfeeblement of the state. The logic is crystal clear: one has to keep intact the essentials of state-centralized authority in order to transform it into an instrument for the implementation of Islamic law.

Bibliography

Amin, M. H. *Guide of the Perplexed Muslim* [Arabic]. Cairo, 1983.
Fadlallah, M. H. *The Meaning of Force in Islam* [Arabic]. Beirut, 1979.

Friedman, M., and E. Sivan. *Religious Radicalism and Politics in the Middle East.* Albany, 1990.

Ghanushi, R. *Collected Articles* [Arabic]. Paris, 1984.

Guenana, N. *The Jihad: An Islamic Alternative in Egypt.* Cairo Papers in Social Sciences/A.U.C. September 1986.

Kepel, G. *The Prophet and the Pharoah.* Berkeley, 1986.

Mayer, T. *Islamic Resurgence in Israel and in the Administered Territories* [Arabic]. Nazareth, 1986.

Manufi, K. *Political Culture of Egyptian Peasants* [Arabic]. Beirut, 1980.

Shapiro, S. *The Hizbollah Social Network.* Unpublished M.A. dissertation. Tel Aviv University, 1987.

Sultan, I. "Survey of the Attitudes of Students and Parents: The Generation Gap." *Egyptian Journal of Social Sciences* [Arabic]. January 1972.

Uways, S. *Cries of the Silent* [Arabic]. Cairo, 1971.

Yasin, A. *La Révolution à l'heure de l'Islam.* Paris, 1981.

Khomeini: A Fundamentalist?

ERVAND ABRAHAMIAN

How did Grand Ayatollah Ruhollah Khomeini become an Imam?
In similar ways as the Holy Prophet Abraham. He carried out
God's Will; destroyed idols; was willing to sacrifice his own son;
rose up against the tyrants; and led the *mostazafin* (oppressed) in
a crusade against their *mostakberin* (oppressors).

A Parliamentary Deputy, *Kayhan-e Hava'e*, 21 June 1989

Introduction

The slippery label "fundamentalist" has been thrown at Ayatollah
Khomeini so often that it has stuck. By the time of his death, he was
being described as the epitome of Islamic fundamentalism not only
by the mass media and the mainstream newspapers, led by the *New
York Times* and the *Washington Post*, but also by the alternative
journals, such as *The Nation* and *In These Times*, and even by
some Middle East specialist. So much so that Khomeini's own followers, finding no such term in Persian or Arabic, have coined a new
word—*bonyadgarayan*—by translating literally the English term
fundamental-ist. This is curious for clerics who relish accusing their
political rivals of being *elteqati* (eclectic) and *gharbzadeh* (contami-
nated with Western plagues)—especially with such deadly "diseases"
as secularism, liberalism, and socialism.

It is not hard to see why the term fundamentalist has received
such wide currency in the West. For conservatives, it is associated
with xenophobia, militancy, and radicalism. For liberals, it implies
extremism, fanaticism, and traditionalism. For radicals, it means
theological obscurantism, social conservatism, even political atav-
ism, and the rejection of Science, History, Modernity, and the En-

lightenment—all with capital letters. For the Khomeinists themselves, it is a self-advertising label claiming that they are the only ones true to the "fundamentals" of Islam, in sharp contrast to others who have been led astray by foreign concepts and historical misinterpretations of the Koran, the Prophet's Hadiths (Traditions), the *shari'a* (Islamic Laws), and the teachings of the Twelve Shia Imams.

Even though the label has stuck—and no doubt future editions of the *Oxford English Dictionary* will describe Khomeini as the quintessential fundamentalist—I would like to argue that transferring this term, with its origins in early twentieth-century American Protestantism, to a contemporary phenomenon in the Muslim Middle East is not so much wrong as misleading, distorting, and confusing. It may describe particular features of Khomeini—even this is debatable—but it certainly does not describe him in totum.

It is not apt on the grounds of both theology and political philosophy. In the realm of theology, the term implies doctrinal inflexibility, rejection of innovation, and going directly to the original texts, bypassing traditional scholarship. Khomeini, however, was a strange combination. On one hand, he insisted that the original texts could not be understood without an intimate knowledge of eleven centuries of Shia scholarship. On the other hand, he was a major theological innovator in that he dared to break with this scholastic tradition to create a brand-new Shia concept of what the state (*dawlat*) should be—one supervised and directed by the *ulama* (clergy) in general and by the leading *fuqaha* (religious jurists) in particular. He defined this state as the *Velayat-e Faqih* (Jurist's Trusteeship). Others call it the "dictatorship of the mullatariat."

In the realm of philosophy, the term fundamentalism implies otherworldliness rather than this-worldliness, revelation rather than science and rationality, moral-religious rejuvenation rather than socioeconomic transformation. It conjures up doctrinal obsession with "moral" concerns—such as abortion, man's creation, and Judgment Day—rather than with such political issues as revolution, imperialism, and social justice. In fact, Khomeini and his disciples succeeded in gaining power in most part because in their public pronouncements they did not dwell on such "fundamentalist" concerns. Instead they hammered the shah with a host of highly sensitive economic, social, and political issues, and, in doing so, developed a new Islam which could be described as the Iranian version of political populism.

Khomeini's populism has more in common with that of Ataturk, Péron, and other Latin American charismatic figures—and even of Hitler, Mussolini, and European fascists—than with traditional Shiism and conventional Islam. They all contained much radical-sounding rhetoric, but no concrete programs for the redistribution of wealth. They all vociferously attacked the political establishment, the comprador bourgeoisie, and the foreign powers, but remained conspicuously silent on the question of middle-class property. They all claimed to be waging war on "international ideas" and returning to "native roots"; but in actual fact they borrowed heavily from the outside world—especially from Marxism, which they perceived as a "cosmopolitan Jewish conspiracy." They saw "foreign plots" everywhere, particularly among ethnic minorities, political dissenters, and university intellectuals. They all used mass institutions and a plebiscite style of politics to mobilize the public, but at the same time distrusted any form of liberalism, political pluralism, and grassroot organizations. What is more, Khomeini's populism—like populism the world over—disparaged democracy, built the state into a behemoth, reveled in the cult of death and martyrdom, and elevated the leader to the status of a demigod towering above the nation. The title *Imam*, which the revolution endowed on Khomeini, reflects this attitude; for, until the 1970s, Iranians considered this title to be sacred and used it only to refer to the Twelve Imams of early Shiism. In fact, the true fundamentalists in Iran consider it blasphemous to use this title for Khomeini.

Khomeini's View of the State

Throughout the Middle Ages the Shia ulama, unlike their Sunni counterparts, failed to develop a consistent theory of the state. The Sunnis, recognizing the Ummayid and the Abbasid caliphs as the Prophet's legitimate successors, accepted the existing power structures as lawful as long as these rulers did not blatantly violate Islamic norms. Had not the Prophet himself said, "My community will never agree on an error"? Had not the Koran commanded: "Obey God, obey His Prophet, and obey those among you who hold authority"? Had not al-Gazzali, the preeminent medieval philosopher, argued that rulers were appointed by God, that rebellion against kings was tanta-mount to rejection of God, and that forty years of bad monarchy were better than one single day of anarchy? Thus the Sunni clergy tended to associate political obedience with religious duty, and civil disobe-dience with religious heresy.

The Shia ulama, however, were more ambivalent. As members of *Shi' al-Ali* (Ali's Party), they believed that the Prophet's true heirs were not the elected and then the hereditary caliphs, but the Twelve Imams—beginning with Ali, the Prophet's son-in-law, first cousin, adopted son, and, according to them, designated successor as the Imam (leader) of the *Ummat* (Muslim community); going through Hosayn, the Third Imam, who, as Ali's son, had rebelled against the usurper Caliph Yazid and had been martyred at the battle of Karbala forty-eight years after the Prophet's death; and ending with the last of Hosayn's direct male descendants, the Twelfth Imam, also known as the *Mahdi* (Messiah), the *Imam-e Montazer* (Expected One), and the *Saheb-e Zaman* (Lord of the Age), who had supposedly gone into occultation some 200 years after Hosayn's martyrdom and would reappear at some future time—when the world was overflowing with corruption and oppression—to prepare the way for Judgment Day.

Although the Shia ulama agreed that only the Hidden Imam had full legitimacy, they sharply disagreed in their attitudes toward the existing states, even when these states were Shia. Some argued that since all temporal rulers were in essence usurpers, true believers should reject the state and always remain mindful of three sacred quotations. The first, a hadith from the Prophet, warned: "When you see a Koran reader seeking shelter with the ruler, know he is a thief." The second, a homily attributed to Imam Ali and found in his much-used *Nahj al-Balaqhah* (Way of Eloquence), declared: "Rulership is like dirty water, not fit for consumption. It is like a morsel which suffocates the person trying to swallow it." The third came from Jafar Sadeq, the Sixth and the most scholarly of the Twelve Imams, who at a time of intense persecution had advised his followers to hate the state and if necessary to obstruct its activities through dissimulation (*taqiyya*). Elaborating on these warnings, some clerics advised their congregations to avoid the state like the plague, decline government offices and favors, treat rulers with suspicion, shun Friday prayers where thanks would be given to the monarch, take disputes to their own legal experts rather than to the state judges, practice dissimulation when endangered by the authorities, and pay *khoms*, the main legitimate tax, not to the government but to the ulama, as the *Nayeb-e Imam* (Imam's deputy).

Other Shia clerics, however, argued that one should accept the state, albeit half-heartedly. They reminded their readers that the Imams, particularly the Fifth, Sixth, and Eighth, had categorically opposed armed insurrections; that Imam Ali, in his *Nahj al-Balaqhah*, had warned of the dangers of "social chaos"; that bad government was better than "no government"; that unjust kings were God's punishment for people's sins; and that Imam Jafar himself had preached: "If your ruler is bad, ask God to reform him, but if he is good, ask God to prolong his life."

Yet others whole-heartedly accepted the state, especially the Shia dynasty set up in Iran by the Safavids in 1501. Following the example of Mohammad Baqer Majlisi, the preeminent Safavid theologian, they argued that kings were shadows of God on earth; that obedience was their divine right; that political dissent led directly to eternal damnation; that believers should not only obey but also eagerly serve the state; that without monarchy there would inevitably be complete social anarchy; and that the monarchy and the clerical hierarchy were complementary pillars of the state since both were equal heirs to the Imam's inheritance. In making these arguments, these clerics often quoted not only al-Ghazzali but also the famous Koranic commandment enjoining the faithful to "obey those who hold authority." In this form the Shia concept of the state was almost the mirror image of that of the conservative Sunnis.

It is significant that in these discussions that went on intermittently for some eleven centuries, no Shia writer actually contended either that the monarchies per se were unacceptable, or that the senior clerics—the grand ayatollahs—had the authority to control the state. Most agreed that the clergy's main responsibilities—referred to by some as the *velayat-e faqih*—were predominantly apolitical. They were to study the law (*fiqh*) based on the Koran, the Prophet's hadiths, and the teaching of the Imams; use *ijtehad* (reason and knowledge of the scriptures) to update these traditional laws and to issue pronouncements (*fatvas*) on new concerns; judicate in disputes between Shia litigants; and distribute the khoms contributions to worthy widows, orphans, seminary students, and indigent *sayyids* (presumed male descendants of the Prophet). In fact, many regarded the term velayat-e faqih as no more than the judicial guardianship of the senior clerics over those deemed incapable of looking after themselves—minors, widows, and the insane. A few went further to argue that if the rulers grossly violated the laws, the senior clerics had the added responsibility of temporarily entering the political arena to protect the Muslim community. For example, when Mohammad Hasan Shirazi—one of the first ayatollahs to be generally recognized as the single most important faqih, the *mar ja'-e taqlid* (Source of Imitation) of his time—led the Tobacco Protest against the Qajar Shah in 1891, he stressed throughout the crisis that he was merely opposed to "bad advisers" and that he would withdraw from politics once the shah cancelled the hated concession. Similarly, the ayatollahs who participated in the constitutional movement of 1905–9 sought neither to overthrow the monarchy nor to establish a theocracy, but at most to set up a supervisory committee of senior clerics to ensure that laws passed by the elected parliament conformed to the shari'a.

Khomeini began his political career with these typical Shia ambiguities toward the state. He published his very first political tract in 1943 when he was a mere thirty-nine-year-old hojjat al-islam. Entitled *Kashf Asrar* (*Secrets Unveiled*), this tract denounced Reza Shah, forced to abdicate two years earlier, for a host of secular sins: closing down seminaries, expropriating religious endowments, propagating "anticlerical attitudes among the masses," replacing shari'a judges with state courts, permitting the consumption of alcoholic beverages and the playing of "sensuous music," forcing men to wear Western-style hats, establishing coeducational schools, and banning the chador, thus "forcing women to go naked into the streets." But no where in this 334-page tract did he call for a revolution against the monarchy. On the contrary, he explicitly disavowed wanting to overthrow the monarchy, and repeatedly reaffirmed his allegiance to monarchies in general and to "good monarchs" in particular. He argued that the clergy had never opposed the state, even when the state issued anti-Islamic orders, for a "bad order was better than no order at all." He emphasized that no faqih had ever claimed the right to rule; that many, including Majlisi, had supported their rulers, participated in governing the country, and encouraged the faithful to pay taxes and cooperate with government functionaries. If, on rare occasions, they had criticized their rulers it was because they opposed individual monarchs, not because they questioned the "principal foundations of monarchy (*saltanat*)." He also reminded his readers that Imam Ali had accepted "even the worst of the early caliphs."[1]

The most Khomeini asked in *Kashf Asrar* was that the monarch should show more respect for the clergy, recruit more of them into parliament, and heed their advice to make sure state laws conformed with the shari'a. For the shari'a, he argued, had prescriptions for all social ills; and the ulama, particularly the fuqaha, being specialists on the shari'a, were like highly trained doctors who knew how to cure these ills.[2]

In concluding *Kashf Asrar*, Khomeini reiterated the mainstream Shia tenet against their more "fundamentalist" Akhbari rivals of earlier centuries, who had argued that any descendant of the Prophet could understand the Word of God, especially the shari'a, by going directly to the main sources—the Koran and the Hadiths. Khomeini countered that some features of God's Word were beyond most people's comprehension and that even Archangel Gabriel had not been able to understand everything he conveyed in the Koran.[3] One should not even attempt to understand the "inner meanings" of the Koran and the Hadiths unless one was familiar with Arabic, knew the teachings of the Twelve Imams, had studied the works of the preceding generations of Shia scholars, and, most nebulous of all, could grasp the "language of *irfan*" (gnostics). Khomeini continued through his life to argue that the Koran and the Hadiths had many different layers. Some could be understood by the average man, some by the ulama who had spent a lifetime studying them, and some by the select few—namely the Imams and those who had in some mysterious way received from them gnostic knowledge.[4] This stress on gnosticism—together with the fact that Khomeini began his teaching career at the Fayzieh Seminary lecturing on mysticism, and throughout his life had high regard for the Naqshbandi Sufi Order—have led some to suspect that Khomeini harbored mystic tendencies. If so, he could hardly be described as a fundamentalist. Besides, Khomeini certainly did not share with Protestant fundamentalists the democratic notion that any true believer could understand the Word of God by going directly to the Scriptures.

Khomeini's attitude toward the state remained conventional even during the 1963 uprising. As a sixty-one-year-old ayatollah, Khomeini raised the banner of opposition to Mohammad Reza Shah from 1962 to 1964, and thereby attained for the first time national prominence recognized by some as their marja'-e taqlid. But even in this bloody confrontation, he called neither for a revolution nor for the overthrow of the monarchy. Instead he castigated the shah for a series of secular and national transgressions: for permitting women to vote in local elections and citizens to take vows on "any sacred book"; for encouraging clerics to stay out of politics and smearing them as "black reactionaries"; and for trampling over the constitutional laws, especially the clause that gave the senior clerics supervisory power over all legislation. He also castigated the shah for supposedly giving high offices to the Bahais; for siding with Israel against the Arabs and thus causing "our Sunni brothers to think that we Shias are really Jews"; and, most sensitive of all, for "capitulating" to the almighty dollar by exempting American personnel from Iranian laws.[5] "An American cook," Khomeini declared, "can now assassinate a maraja'-e taqlid or run over the shah without having to fear our laws."

These castigations, however, were still made in the manner of warning the shah to mend his ways. He again reminded his audience that Imam Ali had accepted the caliphs. He expressed "deep sorrow" that the shah continued to maltreat the ulama who were "the true guardians of Islam." He stressed that he wanted the young shah to reform so he would not go the same way as his father—into exile.[6] And even in 1965—after his own deportation—he continued to accept monarchies as legitimate, for he exhorted Muslim monarchs to work together with Muslim republics against Israel.[7]

Khomeini did not develop a new notion of the state, or of society, until the very late 1960s. It is not clear where the new notions came from. Khomeini refused to admit that he had ever formulated new concepts. He was not in the habit of footnoting his works and giving credit where credit was due, especially if these sources were somewhat "suspect." And in the crucial period of 1965–70, when he was developing his ideas, he was conspicuously silent, rarely giving interviews, sermons, and pronouncements. One can only speculate the source of these new ideas. They may have come from Shia theologians in Iraq where Khomeini resided after 1964. These theologians had been deeply influenced by the local communist party, which had for years played an important role both in Iraqi politics and in the Shia community. They may have come from Khomeini's younger Iranian students, more and more of whom originated in the lower middle class. They may have come from the Iranian intelligentsia—especially Shariati, the Mojahedin, and the Confederation of Iranian Students in Exile, all of whom had been influenced by contemporary Marxism, especially by Maoism and Castroism.

What caused Khomeini to change his ideas is debatable, but the actual changes are undeniable. He broke his long silence in early 1970 by giving in Najaf a series of lectures attacking—without naming names—senior clerics who, he claimed, used the seminaries to escape from political realities. These lectures, originally given in Arabic, were soon published in Persian under the title *Velayat-e Faqih: Hokumat-e Islami* (*The Jurist's Trusteeship: Islamic Government*).[8] In these lectures, Khomeini declared in no uncertain terms that Islam and monarchies (*saltanatha*) were incompatible; that the latter were pre-Islamic institutions which the "despotic" Sunnis, especially the Ummayids, had adopted from the pagan Roman and Iranian empires; that the ancient prophets, particularly Moses, had opposed the pharaohs because they judged such titles to be unlawful; that Imam Hosayn had raised the banner of revolt in Karbala because he had on principle opposed hereditary kingship; that monarchies were tantamount to *taqhut* (false gods), *shirk* (idolatry), and *fasadefi al-arazi* (sowing corruption on earth); and that the Prophet Mohammad had declared "*mulk al-mulk* to be the most hated of all titles in the eyes of God"; Khomeini interpreted this title to be the same as "Shah of Shahs."

Muslims, Khomeini insisted, have the divine duty to rise up (qiyam) against their monarchs. They must not collaborate with them, have recourse to their institutions, subsidize their bureaucracies, and practice dissimulation to conceal their true beliefs. Most kings, he concluded, had been crooks, oppressors, and mass murderers. In later years, he went further to argue that all kings throughout history—including Shah Abbas, the founder of the Shia Safavid dynasty, and Anushirevan, the ancient monarch whom Iranians referred to as the Just—had been without exception thoroughly unjust.[9]

Velayat-e Faqih not only denounced all monarchies but also put forth reasons why the clergy had the divine right to rule.[10] It interpreted the well-known Koranic commandment, "Obey those among you who hold authority," to mean that Muslims had to place themselves under the guidance of the fuqaha. For the Prophet had handed down to the Imams all-encompassing authority—the right to lead and supervise the community as well as to interpret and implement the shari'a. And the Twelfth Imam, in going into occultation, had handed down this encompassing authority to the fuqaha. Had not Imam Ali ordered "all believers to obey his successors"? Had he not explained that by "successors" he meant "those who transmit my statements and my traditions, and teach them to the people"? Had not Imam Musa praised the fuqaha as "the fortress of Islam"? Had not the Twelfth Imam instructed future generations to obey those who knew his teaching, since they were his representatives among believers in the same way he was God's representative among all believers? Had not the Prophet himself said that knowledge led to paradise and that "men of knowledge" had as much superiority over ordinary humans as the full moon had over the stars?

Khomeini also argued that the senior clerics, especially the fuqaha, were the only group with the legitimate expertise to rule. For God had designed the shari'a to guide the community and the state to implement the same shari'a. And since the fuqaha were the only real experts on the shari'a, one had to conclude that they should control the state. The fuqaha, Khomeini insisted, have the "same powers" as the Prophet and the Imams; and the term *velayat-e faqeh* meant jurisdiction not only over minors, widows, and the mentally incompetent, but also over all subjects, in that everyone was in dire need of the shari'a. In other words, disobedience to the fuqaha was the same as disobedience to God. If contemporary Muslims find these obvious conclusions to be "strange," Khomeini repeatedly emphasized, it was because "Jews," "imperialists," and "defective seminaries" had for years spread false propaganda about Islam.[11]

Khomeini's View of Society

Khomeini's view of society developed along parallel lines. His pre-1970 writings reflect the traditional notions of society as sketched out in the Nahj al-Balaqhah, in the teachings of the Shia ulama, and in the "Mirror for Princes" literature produced by the Safavid and Qajar courts. He accepted much of his predecessors' conservative and paternalistic presumptions: that God had created both private property and society; that society was formed of multilayered and mutually dependent classes (tabaqat); that the poor should accept their poverty and not envy the rich; that the rich should thank God, avoid conspicuous consumption, and give generous alms to the unfortunate; that class hatred was sinful, for it led directly to enqelab (revolution), a term he lumped together with chaos and social anarchy; that the shari'a protected wealth as a "divine gift"; and that the state had the duty to maintain a healthy balance among the various classes and to guarantee that no one group transgressed on the rights of others. Some commentators on the Nahj al-Balaghah liked to point out that the Prophet Mohammad had been one of the rich merchants in Mecca.[12]

Khomeini's post-1970 writings, however, depict society as sharply divided between two antagonistic forces: the mostazafin (oppressed) against the mostakberin (oppressors); the fegra (poor) against the sarvatmandan (rich); the mellat-e mostazaf (nation of oppressed) against the hokumat-e shaytan (government of satan); the zakhneshinha (shantytown-dwellers) against the kaghneshinha (palace-dwellers); and the tabaqeh-e payin (lower class) against the tabaqeh-e bala (upper class). The key term mostazafin sums up the transformation. This term had been used in the early Islamic texts, including the Koran, to signify the "weak," the "feeble," the "meek," i.e., orphans, widows, and mental incompetents. Although it had not appeared in

Khomeini's early works, the same word cropped up in almost all of Khomeini's later speeches to describe the broad masses including the small, propertied middle class. In fact, Khomeini's use of the term was reminiscent not only of Fanon's book *Wretched of the Earth* (whose Persian translation employed the word *mostazafin*), but also of the Jacobin concept *sans culottes* and Péron's slogan *descamisados* (shirtless ones).

In depicting society as divided into two warring forces, Khomeini denounced Mohammad Reza Shah on a number of highly sensitive socioeconomic issues. He accused the shah of widening the gap between rich and poor; lining the pockets of relatives, cronies, and senior officials; wasting precious oil resources on the ever-expanding army and bureaucracy; wallowing in luxury while many starved; setting up phoney assembly plants instead of real industrial factories; depriving the countryside of essential services, especially public baths, electricity, schools, and medical clinics; failing to distribute land to the landless peasantry; condemning the working class to a life of poverty, misery, and drudgery; creating huge shantytowns by neglecting to construct low-income housing; bankrupting the bazaars by refusing to protect them against foreign competition and superrich entrepreneurs; and compounding social problems by taking no serious action against prostitution, crime, alcoholism, and drug addiction.[13] Of course, he continued to accuse the shah of allying Iran with the United States; of siding with Israel against the Arab world; of trampling over political liberties, especially the constitution; and of undermining both Islam and Iran with secularism and cultural imperialism.

In these denunciations Khomeini often resorted to populist rhetoric, which, like most populist rhetoric, sounded highly radical. But he silently and intentionally avoided questioning the sanctity of middle-class property. He declared: "Islam belongs to the mostazafin"; "Islam is for equity and social justice"; "a country that has shantytowns is not Islamic"; "we are for Islam, not for Capitalism and Feudalism"; "in a truly Islamic society, there will be no landless peasants"; "Islam will eliminate class differences"; "Islam represents the shantytown-dwellers, not the palace-dwellers"; "the duty of the ulama is to liberate the hungry and the oppressed from the clutches of the rich and the oppressors"; "Islam originates from the masses, not from the upper class"; "the poor were for the Prophet, the rich were against Him"; "the mostazafin died for the Islamic Revolution, the mostakberin plotted against it"; "the martyrs of the Islamic Revolution all came from the lower classes—from the peasantry, the working class, and the bazaar merchants and tradesmen"; "the mostazafin of the world should unite against imperialism"; "the mostazafin of the world should create the Party of the Mostazafin"; "workers and peasants are the two main pillars of national independence"; and, "a day in the life of a worker is more valuable than the whole life of a capitalist exploiter." Khomeini's radical disciples used some of these phrases as potent street slogans.[14]

Khomeini, moreover, reinterpreted early Islamic history to reinforce these populist notions. He argued that the Prophet had been a humble shepherd who had considered the "sweat of a worker to be more valuable than the blood of a martyr"; that Imam Ali had been a hard-working water carrier who had championed the *mazlum* (oppressed) against the *zalem* (oppressors); and that many of the early prophets had been laborers who had looked forward to the day when the "mostazafin would become the mostakberin and the mostakberin would become the mostazafin." He, furthermore, claimed that the Shia ulama, including the grand ayatollahs, had always championed the rights of Iran, kept alive "national consciousness," originated among the common people, died with few worldly possessions, and lived lives as simple as the "lower masses" (*mardom-e payin*).[15]

Khomeini's populist rhetoric reached a crescendo on the eve of the Iranian Revolution. In the last months of the shah's rule, Khomeini began to call for both an *engelab* (revolution) and a *jomhuri* (republic), two terms he had until then scrupulously avoided because of their negative connotations among the traditionalists. He now argued that the Islamic Revolution would pave the way for an Islamic Republic, which, in turn, would eventually bring about the ideal Islamic society. This, being in exact opposition to Pahlavi Iran, would be free of want, hunger, unemployment, slums, poverty, inequality, illiteracy, ignorance, crime, alcoholism, drug addiction, prostitution, nepotism, corruption, oppression, political repression, class exploitation, cultural alienation, and, yes, even of bureaucratic red tape. It would instead be a community based on equality, fraternity, and social justice where there would be no class conflict, no gap between people and state, and no dependency on foreign countries.

In promising utopia, Khomeini managed to discard—first implicitly and in later years explicitly—two important tenets of traditional Shiis. For centuries, Shiis had looked back longingly on Mohammad's Mecca and Imam Ali's caliphate as the Golden Age of Islam. Khomeini now suggested that these early societies had been full of insoluble problems and that revolutionary Iran had already surpassed them in implementing real Islam.[16] For centuries, Shiis had prophesied that the Mahdi would return when the world was overflowing with tyranny, injustice, and oppression. Khomeini now argued that the Mahdi would reappear only when Muslims had returned to Islam, and that true believers could hasten his reappearance by spreading the revolution abroad and by working to establish a truly Islamic society.[17] The traditional quietist tenet had been turned inside out. Khomeini has been praised as an "idol-breaker"; "tradition-breaker" would have been more apt.

Notes

1. R. Khomeini, *Kashf Asrar* (*Secrets Unveiled*) (Tehran: 1943), pp. 1–66, 185–88, 226.

2. Ibid., p. 195.

3. Ibid., p. 322.

4. Khomeini, Speech, *Jomhuri-ye Islami*, 22–31 December 1979; *Ettela'at*, 25 August 1986; *Kayhan-e Hava'i*, 18 November 1987.

5. For Khomeini's speeches and proclamations from 1962 to 1964, see: H. Ruhani (Ziarati), *Nahzat-e Imam Khomeini* (*Imam Khomeini's Movement*) (Teheran: 1980), vol. 1, pp. 142–735; Front for the Liberation of Iran (JAMA), *Khomeini va Jonbesh* (*Khomeini and the Movement*), N.p. (1973), pp. 1–35.

6. Ruhani, *Nahzat-e*, pp. 195, 198, 458.

7. Ibid., vol. 2, p. 159.

8. R. Khomeini, *Velayat-e Faqih: Hokumat-e Islami* (Tehran: 1977).

9. R. Khomeini, Speech, *Ettela'at*, 2 December 1985.

10. Khomeini, *Velayat-e Faqih*, pp. 67–127.

11. Ibid., pp. 65–67, 106, 6–7, 24, 85.

12. S. M. Askari Jafery, trans., *Nahjul Balagha* (New York: 1981), pp. 13, 124.

13. For Khomeini's speeches on these issues, see Ruhani, *Nahzat-e,* vol 1; JAMA; *Khabarnameh,* 1972–79; *Payam-e Mojahed,* 1972–78.

14. See "The Mostazafin and the Mostakberin," *Ettela'at,* 15 February–23 April 1983.

15. R. Khomeini, Speech, *Iran Times,* 27 May 1983.

16. R. Khomeini, Speech, *Ettela'at,* 28 December 1979; *Iran Times,* 4 December 1982; *Kayhan-e Hava'i,* 9 May 1984.

17. R. Khomeini, Speech, *Ettela'at,* 13 April 1988; *Iran Times,* 27 March 1982.

Bibliography

Abrahamian, E. *The Iranian Mojahedin.* New Haven: Yale University Press, 1989.

Akhavan-Towhidi, H. *Dar Pars-e Pardeh-e Tazvir (Behind the Veils of Dissimulation).* Paris: N.p., 1984.

Akhavi, S. "The Ideology and Praxis of Shi'ism in the Iranian Revolution." *Comparative Studies in Society and History* 25, no. 2 (April 1983): 195–221.

———. "Islam, Politics and Society in the Thought of Ayatullah Khomeini, Ayatullah Taliqani and Ali Shariati." *Middle Eastern Studies* 24, no. 4 (October 1988): 404–31.

———. *Religion and Politics in Contemporary Iran.* Albany, N.Y.: State University of New York Press, 1980.

Algar, H. *Islam and Revolution: Writings and Declarations of Imam Khomeini.* Berkeley: Mizan Press, 1981.

Arjomand, S. "The State and Khomeini's Islamic Order." *Iranian Studies* 13, nos. 1–4 (1980): 147–64.

———. *The Turban for the Crown.* New York: Oxford University Press, 1988.

———, ed. *Authority and Political Culture in Shi'ism.* Albany, N.Y.: State University of New York Press, 1988.

———. *From Nationalism to Revolutionary Islam.* Albany, N.Y.: State University of New York Press, 1984.

Bakhash, S. "Islam and Social Justice in Iran." In *Shi'ism, Resistance, and Revolution,* ed. E. Kramer. Boulder, Colo.: Westview Press, 1987, pp. 95–115.

———. "The Politics of Land, Law, and Social Justice in Iran." *Middle East Journal* 43, no. 2 (Spring 1989): 186–201.

———. *The Reign of the Ayatollahs.* New York: Basic Books, 1984.

Bayat, G. "The Iranian Revolution of 1978: Fundamentalist or Modern?" *Middle East Journal* 37, no. 1 (Winter 1983): 30–42.

————. "Taleqani and the Iranian Revolution." In *Shi'ism, Resistance, and Revolution*, ed. E. Kramer. Boulder, Colo.: Westview Press, 1987, pp. 67–93.

Bill, J. "Power and Religion in Revolutionary Iran." *Middle East Journal* 36, no. 1 (Winter 1982): 22–47.

Calder, N. "Accommodation and Revolution in Imami Shi'i Jurisprudence." *Middle Eastern Studies* 18, no. 1 (January 1982): 1–20.

Cole, J., and N. Keddie. *Shi'ism and Social Protest*. New Haven: Yale University Press, 1986.

Eliash, J. "Misconceptions Regarding the Juridical Status of the Iranian Ulama." *International Journal of Middle East Studies* 10, no. 1 (February 1979): 9–25.

Enayat, H. "Iran: Khumayni's Concept of the Guardianship of the Jurisconsult." In *Islam in the Political Process*, ed. J. Piscatori. New York: Cambridge University Press, 1983, pp. 160–80.

————. *Modern Islamic Political Thought*. London: Macmillan Press, 1982.

Ferdows, A. "Khomaini and Fedayan's Society and Politics." *International Journal of Middle East Studies*, 15, no. 2 (May 1983): 241–57.

Fischer, M. "Imam Khomeini: Four Levels of Understanding." In *Voices of Resurgent Islam*. New York: Oxford University Press, 1983, pp. 150–74.

————. *Iran: From Religious Dispute to Revolution*. Cambridge: Harvard University Press, 1980.

Front for the Liberation of Iran (JAMA), *Khomeini va Jonbesh (Khomeini and the Movement)*. Tehran: Moharram Press, 1973.

Hairi, A. "The Legacy of the Early Qajar Rule as Viewed by the Shi'i Religious Leaders." *Middle Eastern Studies* 24, no. 3 (July 1988): 271–86.

Halliday, F. "The Iranian Revolution: Uneven Development and Religious Populism." In *State and Ideology in the Middle East and Pakistan*, ed. F. Halliday and H. Alavi. New York: Monthly Review Press, 1988, pp. 31–64.

Hooglund, E. "Rural Iran and the Clerics." *Merip*, no. 104 (March–April 1982): 23–26.

————. "Social Origins of the Revolutionary Clergy." In *The Iranian Revolution and the Islamic Republic*, ed. N. Keddie and E. Hooglund. Syracuse, N.Y.: Syracuse University Press, 1986.

Kazemi, F., ed. *Iranian Revolution in Perspective* (Special issue of *Iranian Studies*). Boston: Iranian Studies, 1981.

Keddie, N. *Religion and Politics in Iran*. New Haven: Yale University Press, 1983.

————. *Roots of Revolution*. New Haven: Yale University Press, 1981.

Khomeini, R. *Kashf Asrar* (Secrets Unveiled). Tehran: N.p., 1943.

————. *Towzeh al-Masail* (Questions Clarified). Tehran: N.p., 1978.

———. *Velayat-e Faqih: Hokumat-e Islami* (The Jurist's Trusteeship: Islamic Government). Tehran: N.p., 1977.

Lambton, A. "A Reconsideration of the Position of the Marja' al-Taqlid." *Studia Islamica* 20 (1964): 115–35.

Loeffler, L. *Islam in Practice.* Albany, N.Y.: State University of New York Press, 1988.

McEoin, D. "Aspects of Militancy and Quietism in Imami Shi'ism." *Bulletin of the British Society of Middle East Studies* 11, no. 1 (1984): 18–27.

Menashri, D. "Shi'i Leadership." *Iranian Studies* 13 (1980): 119–46.

Moaddel, M. "The Shi'i Ulama and the State in Iran." *Theory and Society* 15 (1986): 519–56.

Mottahedeh, R. *The Mantle of the Prophet.* New York: Simon and Schuster, 1985.

Rajaee, F. *Islamic Values and World View.* New York: University Press of America, 1983.

Ruhani, H. *Nahzat-e Imam Khomeini (Imam Khomeini's Movement),* vols. 1–2. Tehran: Imam's Way Press, 1984.

Savory, R. "Ex Oriente Nebula." In *Ideology and Power in the Middle East,* ed. P. Chelkowski and R. Pranger. Durham, N.C.: Duke University Press, 1988, pp. 339–64.

Sivan, E. "Sunni Radicalism in the Middle East and the Iranian Revolution." *International Journal of Middle East Studies* 21, no. 1 (February 1989): 1–30.

Tehran University Publication Center. *Mosahebehha-ye Imam Khomeini* (Imam Khomeini's Interviews). Tehran: Tehran University Press, 1983.

Zonis, M. and D. Brumber. *Khomeini, the Islamic Republic of Iran and the Arab World.* Cambridge: Harvard Middle East Center, 1987.

Zubaida, S. "An Islamic State: The Case of Iran." *Merip,* no. 153 (July–August 1988): 3–7.

———. "The Quest for the Islamic State." In *Studies in Religious Fundamentalism,* ed. L. Caplan. Albany, N.Y.: State University of New York Press, 1987, pp. 25–50.

7

Fundamentalism and the Woman Question in Afghanistan

VALENTINE M. MOGHADAM

Introduction

During the 1980s, Afghanistan was the site of a prolonged and bloody battle between government forces, who were assisted by Soviet troops, and an armed Islamist opposition collectively known as the Mujahideen, which was supported by Pakistan, the United States, Saudi Arabia, and the Islamic Republic of Iran. The geopolitical dimension of the conflict—and international opprobrium for the Soviet military intervention—overshadowed two important issues: (1) the origins of the conflict between right-wing Islamists and the left-wing government, and (2) the importance of "the woman question" to the conflict. It is my contention that the Soviet intervention and world attention to it obscured the essential nature of the conflict: between modernizers and traditionalists, and between women's emancipation and patriarchy.

This essay focuses on the woman question in Afghanistan, in particular the vexing issue of women's rights and women's emancipation. It surveys the status of Afghan women before and after the Saur Revolution of April 1978, comparing the situation of women under the government in Kabul with that under the Mujahideen in the refugee camps of Peshawar, Pakistan. Notwithstanding the neglect of the

126

gender dimension in nearly all accounts of Afghanistan, the woman question was an integral part of the conflict between the Mujahideen and the People's Democratic Party of Afghanistan (PDPA), the ruling party which came to power in the Saur Revolution.

Recent feminist scholarship has revealed the centrality of the woman question during periods of social change or political contest (Yuval-Davis and Anthias 1989; Moghadam 1990, 1991). Women frequently become the symbol or marker of political goals and cultural identity during processes of revolution and state-building, and when power is being contested or reproduced. Representatives of women are deployed, including the unveiled woman of today, who signifies modernity and national progress, or the veiled, domesticated woman, who symbolizes authenticity and the cultural reproduction of the group. Women's behavior and appearance—and the range of their activities—come to be defined by, and are frequently subject to, the political or cultural objectives of political movements, states, and leaderships. In some political projects, women may be linked to modernization and progress (as in the case of Turkey under Ataturk, Tunisia under Bourguiba, South Yemen under Marxist leadership, and Afghanistan under the PDPA). In other political projects, women are linked to cultural rejuvenation and religious orthodoxy (as in the case of Iran under Ayatollah Khomeini, Pakistan under Zia ul-Haq, the Afghan Mujahideen). In patriarchal contexts in particular, where women's reproductive roles are fetishized in the context of kinship-ordered structures, women must also assume the burden of maintaining, representing, and transmitting cultural values and traditions.

This essay considers the importance of the women's rights issue in recent Afghan history, and the battle over "the woman question" between fundamentalists and reformers. The issue of women's rights in Afghanistan has historically been constrained by (1) the patriarchal nature of gender and social relations, deeply embedded in traditional communities, and (2) the existence of a weak central state, which since at least the beginning of this century has been unable to fully implement modernizing programs and goals. The two are interconnected, for the state's weakness is correlated with a strong (if fragmented) society resistant to state bureaucratic expansion, civil authority, regulation, monopoly of the means of violence, and extraction—the business of modern states. Today's Afghan state is arguably stronger than it has been in the past, and some important steps were taken during the late 1970s and 1980s to improve women's legal status and social positions. Yet war and the fundamentalist backlash have largely defeated the original goal of emancipating Afghan women. In the late 1980s, the Afghan leadership shifted from social revolution to national reconciliation, relegating women's emancipation to a more stable future.

Afghan Social Structure and Its Implications for Women

Historically, the population of Afghanistan has been fragmented into myriad ethnic, linguistic, religious, kin-based, and regional groupings (Dupree 1980; Roy 1986). One of the few commonalities in this diverse country is Islam. Afghan Islam is a unique combination of practices and precepts from the *shari'a* (Islamic canon law as delineated in religious texts) and tribal customs, particularly Pushtunwali (Griffiths 1981: 111–12). For example, contrary to an Islamic ban on usury, it continues to be widespread and has kept rural households in perpetual indebtedness (Griffiths 1981: 122; Male 1982; Hammond 1984: 71; Anwar 1988; Urban 1988: 20). Exorbitant expenditure in marriages (*sheer-baha*) has also contributed to the rural household's debt accumulation. The Islamic dower, *mahr*, has been rendered a brideprice. The absence of inheritance rights for females, though contrary to Islamic law, is integral to the complex web of the tribal exchange system (Tapper 1984; Howard-Merriam 1987).

"Afghan nationalism," properly speaking, is at best incipient, in that the concept of a nation-state or of a national identity is absent for much of the population (Hammond 1984: 5; Urban 1988: 204), having been promoted primarily by modernizing elites since the nineteenth century (Gregorian 1969). During most of the country's recent history, the fragmented groupings composed warring factions. Battles were fought principally over land and water, sometimes over women and "honor," and usually to exhibit sheer power.

Afghanistan's rugged physical environment serves to isolate residential communities and to create microenvironments. Members of the same ethnic group and tribe who reside in different locations must adapt to their own microenvironment, which may result in different kin-based groups within the same tribe and ethnic group using different modes of production. For example, the Durrani Pushtuns—whom Nancy Tapper studied—were primarily agriculturalists, while the Sheikhanzai Durrani Pushtuns, who were the subject of Bahram Tavakolian's research, were primarily pastoralists (Nyrop and Seekins 1986: 105).

In many parts of the Third World, preindustrial modes of production combined with the social and political control that men have over women's lives create a cultural matrix in which men exchange women and control women's productive and reproductive capacities within the family unit. This authority, which is based on patrilineal and kinship relationships, is not diminished by women's central role in agricultural production. Indeed, in some cases women's participation in socially productive work may result in their "enslavement rather than their liberation" (Afshar 1985: 67). What Afshar means is that in such a context, a woman's labor power is controlled and allocated by someone other than herself, the products of her labor are managed by others, and she receives no remuneration for work performed. The partial penetration of capital in rural areas, where, for example, carpet-making is a commercial enterprise, allows male kin to exploit women's labor without any wage payment. Here women's subordination and intrahousehold inequality are intensified as a direct result of their ability to contribute substantially to the family income (Papanek 1985). In many such contexts, women may be seen as "too valuable" to educate and the money they earn may well finance the education of men. For both economic and ideological reasons, females may not be given "release time" for education or labor market employment. In extended patriarchal, patrilineal households, collective (male) interests dictate strict control of female labor deployment throughout a woman's lifetime.

Contemporary Afghanistan is one of the last remaining examples of classic patriarchy. Kandiyoti (1988) refers to "a belt of classic patriarchy" which stretches from northern Africa across the Middle East to the northern plains of the Indian subcontinent and parts of (rural) China. The key to the reproduction of classic patriarchy today lies in the operations of the patrilocally extended household, which is also commonly associated with the reproduction of the peasantry in agrarian societies. The subordination of women in kinship-ordered or agrarian societies seems to be linked to the reproduction of the kin group or of the peasantry, as well as to the sexual division of labor. A predisposition to male dominance is inherent in the relation between the precapitalist peasant household and the world of landlords and the state (Wood 1988), and in the reproduction of kinship-ordered groups, wherein women are exchanged and men are the transactors (Rubin 1975). In a patriarchal context, women are assimilated into concepts of property.

In those areas of the world still characterized by the patriarchal extended family, the senior male has authority over everyone else, including younger men, and women are subject to distinct forms of control and subordination. Indeed, the social structures in the patriarchal belt are characterized by their institutionalization of extremely restrictive codes of behavior for women—such as the practice of rigid gender segregation and a powerful ideology linking family honor to female virtue. Men are entrusted with safeguarding family honor through their control over female members; they are backed by complex social arrangements which ensure women's protection—and dependence (Kabeer 1988: 95). In contemporary Muslim patriarchal societies, such control over women is considered necessary, in part because women are regarded as the potential source of social *fitna*, that is, disorder or anarchy (Sabbah 1984; Ghoussoub 1987).

As Stacey (1983) found, patriarchy in China originates in "a family and social system in which male power over women and children derives from the social role of fatherhood, and is supported by a political economy in which the family unit retains a significant productive role." Young brides marry into large families, gain respect mainly via their sons, and late in life acquire power as mothers-in-law. Women's life-chances are circumscribed by patriarchal arrangements which favor men. One typically finds an adverse sex ratio; low female literacy and educational attainment, high fertility rates, high maternal mortality rates, and low female labor force participation in the formal sector. Demographic facts about societies such as Afghanistan, Pakistan, and north India suggest "a culture against women," in which women are socialized to sacrifice their health, survival chances, and options (Papanek 1989).

The French ethnologist Germaine Tillion (1983) has pointed out that Mediterranean peoples (including Muslims) favor endogamy, and endogamy increases the tendency to control women in tightly interrelated lineages. Nikki Keddie (1989) writes that nomadic tribal groups have special reasons to want to control women and to favor cousin marriage. Pastoral nomadic tribes, the most common type in the Middle East, trade animal products for agricultural and urban ones. The cohesion of tribes and subtribes is necessary to their economy, which requires frequent group decisions about migration. To make decisions amicably, groups closely tied by kin are desirable. The practical benefits of close kinship, Keddie argues, are surely one reason cousin marriage has long been preferred among Middle Eastern people: it encourages family integration and cooperation. Keddie feels that controls on women are connected to the pervasiveness of tribal structures in the Middle East, and notes that even though most nomadic women are not veiled and secluded, they are controlled (Keddie 1989: 7). It is likely that as rural areas are commercialized and social relations are monetized, first-cousin marriages will wane and girls will be married to distant relatives or exchanged for goods or money exogenously. When families seek higher status, girls assume a heavy responsibility.

Afghan patriarchy is tied to the prevalence of such forms of subsistence as nomadic pastoralism, herding and farming, and settled agriculture, all organized along patrilineal lines. Historically, Afghan gender roles and women's status have been tied to property relations. Property includes livestock, land, and houses or tents. Women and children tend to be assimilated into the concept of property and to belong to a male (Anwar 1988; Griffiths 1967; Male 1982; Nyrop and Seekins 1986; Tapper 1984). Gender segregation and female seclusion exist, though they vary by ethnic group, region, mode of subsistence, social class, and family. Few accounts exist of how and to what degree women veil. Among Ghilzai, women veil or are secluded from men to whom they could be married. Men also avoid women who stand in the relationship of potential mate to them (Nyrop and

Seekins 1986: 127). Among the Pushtuns studied by one anthropologist, a bride who does not exhibit signs of virginity on the wedding night may be murdered by her father and/or brothers. This is not the case, however, within the Paghmanis and Absarinas, smaller ethnic groups studied by the same anthropologist (Nyrop and Seekins 1986: 127).

Writing in the mid-1960s, Griffiths (1967) maintained that "the most strikingly obvious divisions in Afghanistan are between the sexes." Inequality is enshrined in the system of purdah, not merely the meaning of the all-encompassing *chadhuri,* but the segregation of women from men, their isolation and seclusion (Lajoinie 1980). Griffiths (1967:78) also describes a conversation with the governor of a district in Kunduz,

> who explained with some pride the way in which the region's beautiful hand-woven carpets were made; how five or six women might work together for four or five months to make a patterned carpet . . . and how a man would pay a very good bride-price for a girl who was an accomplished carpet weaver. When I asked him who got the money for the carpets, he looked at me in astonishment and replied: "Why the man of course; the woman belongs to the man." This is the attitude which is the chief obstacle facing the champions of women's emancipation in Afghanistan.

A small number of female scholars have examined Afghan women's lives. Boesen (1983) reports that women resent male control of their sexuality and rebel, pursuing extramarital affairs and covering up each other's activities. Such forms of resistance, however, do not challenge gender status ranking. Men and women's objectives and lifestyles are in sharp contrast. Nancy Tapper distills Pashtun nomad women's aim in life to a simple wish, which is probably shared by a majority of the country's women: "The principal goal in life is a successful marriage with many sons." (Shalinsky, however, contends that Uzbek women may also wish for many daughters because of greater mother-daughter love and rapport.) In contrast, men are expected to be sexually incontinent. They gain prestige by having illicit sex with women in other men's charge and lost prestige when men have illicit sex with women in their charge (Nyrop and Seekins 1986: 128).

The threat to entrenched patriarchal gender relations posed by various state initiatives during this century has invariably resulted in tribal rebellion against government authority. Gregorian (1969) describes opposition to the modernizing efforts—including education for girls—of Habibullah Khan (1901–19) and Amanullah Khan (1919–29). Other authors have noted persistent government difficulty in extending education to girls (Griffiths 1967, 1981; Hammond 1984; Bradsher 1985; Urban 1988). The existence of a weak modern state in a predominantly patriarchal and tribal society has adverse implications for reform and development, as well as for the advancement of women. Throughout the twentieth century, the state—small and weak as it was—was incapable of effectively implementing its program. Faced with what Gregorian, writing in the late 1960s, frequently referred to as the "staggering socioeconomic problems" of the country, and to the religious-traditionalist forces who have prevented their full transformation, the reformers of 1978 impatiently wished for change and betterment, assisted by their Soviet neighbors. All social and economic indicators announced the need for change, especially in the areas of literacy, education, health, food production and distribution, and infrastructural development. Afghanistan is (and was before 1978) among the poorest countries of the world, with low life expectancy, high child mortality, widespread illiteracy, malnutrition, and an unproductive agricultural system.

Characteristics of Afghan Patriarchy

The exchange of women in precapitalist agrarian societies organized around kinship structures has been extensively discussed in anthropological and feminist literature (Levi-Strauss 1969; Rubin 1976; Lerner 1986). The concept of "honor" in patriarchal societies has similarly been elaborated (Abu-Lughod 1985; Bourdieu 1965; Knauss 1987; Minces 1982; Utas 1983). Both are important elements in Pushtunwali, the dominant Afghan tribal culture. Its elements are highly masculinist. Tapper (1984) reports that the Durrani Pashtuns of north-central Afghanistan "discuss control of all resources—especially labor, land, and women—in terms of honor" (see also Boesen 1983; Nyrop and Seekins 1986: 126–28). Note that "community" is the community of men.

It should also be noted that on certain areas Pushtunwali and Islam disagree (Boesen 1983; Anwar 1988). In the Afghan patriarchal context, brideprice (called *vulver* in Pushtu) was the payment to the bride's father as compensation for the loss of his daughter's labor in the household unit. It is important to distinguish *vulver* from *mahr*. The latter, a payment due from groom to bride, is an essential part of the formal Islamic marriage contract. In the Qoran it is a nominal fee, but in many Muslim countries its purpose is to provide a kind of social insurance for the wife in the event of divorce or widowhood. Thus, Iranian *mahr* differs in meaning and content from the Pushtun *vulver*. In a combination of pre-Islamic and Islamic customs, men exercise control over women in two crucial ways: their control of marriage and of property—as illustrated by the institution of brideprice, the Pushtun prohibition of divorce (and this despite the Quranic allowances, primarily to the men), and the taboo of land ownership for women (again contrary to Islamic law and the actual practice in many other Muslim countries).

In Afghanistan, marriage, enforced or otherwise, was a way to end feuds, cement a political alliance between families, or increase the family's prestige. Women are also regarded as men's property. In the language of functionalist anthropology, women are given for brideprice or in compensation for blood, and this "maintains a status hierarchy" among the households. In the exchange system, men are ranked in the first and highest sphere. Direct exchanges between them include the most honorable and manly of all activities, which are prime expressions of status equality: vengeance and feud, political support and hospitality, and the practice of sanctuary. Women belong to the second sphere; they are often treated exclusively as reproducers and pawns in economic and political exchanges. There is only one proper conversion between the first two spheres: two or more women can be given in compensation for the killing or injury of one man. Mobility and migration patterns also revolve around the brideprice. For example, men from one region will travel to another to find inexpensive brides, while other men will travel elsewhere because they can obtain a higher price for their daughters (Tapper 1984: 304).

Interethnic hostility among Afghans has been widely discussed in the literature (Canfield 1989; Nyrop and Seekins 1986: 112–13; Magnus 1988). Tapper (1984) describes ethnic identity in terms of claims to religiously privileged descent and superiority to all other ethnic groups. Interethnic competition extends to the absolute prohibition on the marriage of Durrani women to men who are of a "lower" ethnic status.

Studies on Pushtunwali note that the code of Afghan behavior among the Pushtuns, who comprise over 50 percent of the population, possesses three core elements: hospitality, refuge, and revenge. Other key values are equality, respect, pride, bravery, purdah (seclusion of women), pursuit of romantic encounters, worship of God, and devoted love for a friend (Griffiths 1981: 111–12; Howard-Merriam 1987; Nyrop and Seekins 1986; Boesen 1983). These are, once again, male values. Purdah is a key element in protecting the family's pride and honor, and Boesen has noted a Pushtun saying that "a woman is best either in the house or in the grave" (Boesen 1983). This seclusion from the world outside the family walls is customarily justified by invoking Quranic prescription and by the notion that women are basically licentious and tempt men. Howard-Merriam (1987) explains that women are regarded as subordinates who depend on their husbands, as further exemplified by the fact that women never ask men their whereabouts or expect marital fidelity. Women also are expected to give all the meat, choicest food, and best clothing to their husbands, as well as their personal wealth if so demanded. Census and surveys undertaken in 1967, 1972–74, and 1979 have revealed an unusually high ratio of males to females, which exceeds even the expected underreporting of females in a conservative Islamic society. This is in part explained by a high rate of maternal mortality (Nyrop and Seekins 1986: 86; Howard-Merriam 1987: 114).

Since a woman's standing is maintained primarily through bearing sons to continue the family, she of course must marry, for in the context of classic patriarchy, only through marriage can one's basic needs be legitimately fulfilled. The choice of husband is made by her family with its own concerns for lineage maintenance or gain and property. The best she can hope for is a handsome and kind cousin or close relative she has known and with whom she has grown up. The worst is an old man from another village whom she has never seen and who is unkind. In either case he is obliged to provide for her materially and, it is to be hoped, father her sons who will endow her with status in her new home. If the husband treats her unbearably, she does have the right to return to her own family or seek refuge with another family. This weapon is not used often, however, as her natal family has given up rights to her through the brideprice at the time of marriage (Howard-Merriam 1987: 106).

Since modernization began in the mid-nineteenth century, various governments and rulers have sought to discourage excessive expenditure not only on brideprice but also on marriage celebrations which add to the rural population's indebtedness. Gregorian (1969) treats this subject in the most detail for the period 1860–1940. Dupree (1980) describes a 1950 law banning "ostentatious life-crises ceremonies;" it prohibited many of the expensive aspects of birth, circumcision, marriage, and burial rituals, but was difficult to enforce. The Marriage Law of 1971 was a further attempt to curb the indebtedness that arises from the costs of marriage which "are a burden for Afghan society as a whole." Tapper (1984) agrees that the heaviest expenses any household has to bear are concerned with marriage. The choice of a bride, the agreed brideprice, and the time taken to complete a marriage may visibly confirm or increase a household's poverty.

An Afghan who devoted his 1976 doctoral dissertation to matrimonial problems described them thus (quoted in Tapper 1984):

> Excessive expenditure in marriage undermines the human dignity of women as it tends to render them into a kind of property of the husband or his family. [It] weakens the financial status of the family and tends to bring or worsen poverty. [It] tends to render the adults highly dependent on family resources; this in turn weakens their position in regard to the exercise of their right of consent in marriage as well as their freedom of choice of a life partner.

The author continues:

> Dependence of the youth on the family resources is enormous even without the stimulus of this additional factor. Marriage becomes largely dependent on the possession of financial means; this leads to intolerable discriminations against the poor. Excessive expenditure in marriage de-

prives many of the right to marry (e.g., many women); it also leads to late marriages, and often brings about a wide disparity of age between the spouses. Excessive expenditure in marriage constitutes a source of embitterment and conflict during the course of marital life. . . . Costly marriages contribute to the continuance of the tradition-bound society and tend to slow down the process of reform. . . . The practice is self-perpetuating.

Such were the practices that concerned the reformers.

The Saur Revolution and Women's Rights

In April 1978, the People's Democratic Party of Afghanistan (PDPA), having seized power in what has been called the Saur (April) Revolution, introduced rapid reforms to change the political and social structure of Afghan society, including patterns of land tenure and gender relations. The government of President Noor Mohammad Taraki enacted legislation to raise women's status through changes in family law—including practices and customs related to marriage—and policies to encourage female education and employment. As in other modernizing and socialist experiments, "the woman question" constituted an essential part of the political project. The Afghan state was motivated by a modernizing outlook and socialist ideology which linked Afghan backwardness to feudalism, widespread female illiteracy, and the exchange of girls. The leadership resolved that women's rights to education, employment, mobility, and choice of spouse would be a major objective of the "national democratic revolution."

Along with land redistribution, the cancellation of peasants' debts and mortgages, and other measures to wrest power from traditional leaders in Afghan society, the government promulgated Decree No. 7 to fundamentally change the institution of marriage. A prime concern of the designers of the decree, which also motivated other reforms of the Taraki government, was to reduce material indebtedness throughout the country; it was further meant to ensure equal rights of women with men. In a speech on 4 November 1978, President Taraki declared: "Through the issuance of decrees no. 6 and 7, the hard-working peasants were freed from bonds of oppressors and money-lenders, ending the sale of girls for good as hereafter nobody would be entitled to sell any girl or woman in this country" (quoted in Tapper 1984).

The first two articles in Decree No. 7 forbade the exchange of a woman in marriage for cash or kind and the payment of other presta-tions customarily due from a bridegroom on festive occasions; the third article set an upper limit of 300 afghanis (the equivalent of $24) on the *mahr*. Articles 4 to 6 of the decree set the ages of first engage-ment and marriage at sixteen for women and eighteen for men; stipulated that no one, including widows, could be compelled to marry against his or her will; stated that no one could be prevented from marrying if she or he so desired (Griffiths 1981; Male 1982; Hammond 1984; Tapper 1984; N. H. Dupree 1984; Bradsher 1985; Anwar 1988). Along with the promulgation of Decree No. 7, the PDPA government embarked upon an aggressive literacy campaign. This was led by the Democratic Women's Organization of Afghanis-tan (DWOA), whose function was to educate women, bring them out of seclusion, and initiate social programs (Nyrop and Seekins 1986: 128). Throughout the countryside, PDPA cadre established literacy classes for men, women, and children in villages. And by August 1979, the government had established 600 new schools. The PDPA's rationale for pursuing the rural literacy campaign with some zeal was that all previous reformers had made literacy a matter of choice. Because male guardians had chosen not to allow their females to be educated, 99 percent of all Afghan women were illiterate. It was therefore decided that literacy was no longer to remain a matter of (men's) choice, but rather a matter of principle and law.

This was, clearly, an audacious program for social change, one aimed at the rapid transformation of a patriarchal society and de-centralized power structure based on tribal and landlord authority. Revolutionary change, state-building, and women's rights subse-quently went hand-in-hand. The emphasis on women's rights on the part of the PDPA reflected: (a) their socialist/Marxist ideology, (b) their modernizing and egalitarian outlook, (c) their social base and origins—urban, middle-class professionals, educated in the United

States, the Soviet Union, and Western and Eastern Europe, and (d) the number and position of women within the PDPA. A brief digression about these women reformers is in order, as it also puts the PDPA project in its social and gender perspective.

Among the most remarkable and influential female reformer was Anahita Ratebzad. In the 1950s she studied nursing in the United States, and then returned to Kabul as director and instructor of nursing at the Women's Hospital. Nancy Dupree notes that when the Faculty for Women at Kabul University was established, Anahita entered the medical college and became a member of its teaching staff upon graduating in 1963. She joined the PDPA in 1965, and along with three other women ran as a candidate for parliament. This was the first time liberals and leftists had openly appeared in the political arena. They were up against the conservative members of parliament who, in 1968, proposed to enact a law prohibiting Afghan girls from studying abroad. Hundreds of girls demonstrated in opposition. In 1970 two reactionary mullahs protested public evidence of female liberation—such as miniskirts, women teachers, and schoolgirls—by shooting at the legs of women in Western dress and splashing them with acid. Among those who joined in this action was Gulbeddin Hekmatyar (who went on to become a leading figure in the Mujahideen, one of the "freedom fighters" hailed by President Reagan). This time there was a protest demonstration of 5,000 girls (N. H. Dupree 1984).

In 1976 Anahita was elected to the cental committee of the PDPA. Following the Saur Revolution, she was elected to the Revolutionary Council of the Democratic Republic of Afghanistan (DRA) and appointed minister of social affairs. Other influential PDPA women in the Taraki government (April 1978–September 1979) were Sultana Umayd, director of Kabul Girls' School; Soraya, president of the DOAW; Ruhafza Kamyar, principal of the DOAW's Vocational High School; Firouza, director of the Afghan Red Crescent (Red Cross); Dilara Mahak, principal of the Amana Fidawa School; and Professor Mrs. R. S. Siddiqui (who was especially outspoken in her criticism of "feudalistic patriarchal relations"). In the Amin government (September–December 1979), the following women headed schools and the women's organization, as well as sat on government subcommit-tees: Fawjiyah Shahsawari, Dr. Aziza, Shirin Afzal, Alamat Tolqun.

These were the women behind the program for women's rights. Their spirit was reflected in an editorial in the *Kabul Times* (5/28/78) which asserted: "privileges which women, by right, must have are equal education, job security, health services, and free time to rear a healthy generation for building the future of this country. . . . Educat-ing and enlightening women is now the subject of close government scrutiny" (quoted in N. H. Dupree 1984).

Patriarchal Resistance to Change

PDPA's attempts to change marriage laws, expand literacy, and edu-cate rural girls met with strong opposition. Decrees 6 and 7 deeply angered the rural tribesmen and the traditional power structure. Believing that women should not appear at public gatherings, vil-lagers often refused to attend classes after the first day (Katsikas 1982: 231). Because the PDPA cadre viewed this attitude as retro-grade, the cadre resorted to different forms of persuasion—including physical force—to make the villagers return to literacy classes. Of-ten the PDPA cadre were either kicked out of the village or murdered. In the summer of 1978 refugees began pouring into Pakistan, giving as their major reason the forceful implementation of the literacy program among their women. In Kandahar, three literacy workers from the women's organization were killed as symbols of the un-wanted revolution. Two men killed all the women in their families to prevent them from "dishonor" (N. H. Dupree 1984).

There was also universal resistance to the new marriage regula-tions which, coupled with compulsory education for girls, raised the threat that women would refuse to obey and submit to family (male) authority. Land reform, cancellation of peasants' debts, and marriage reform threatened vested rural interests and patriarchal structures. The large landowners, the religious establishment, and moneylend-ers were especially appalled at the prospect of social structural trans-formation. An Islamist opposition began organizing and conducted several armed actions against the government in the spring of 1979. Thus, over a year prior to the Soviet military intervention, reaction developed to the government's program for land reform and women's rights.

Internal battles within the PDPA (especially between its two wings, Parcham and Khalq) contributed to the government's difficulties. In September 1979 President Taraki was killed on the orders of his deputy, Hafizullah Amin, a ruthless and ambitious man who imprisoned and executed hundreds of his own comrades in addition to further alienating the population (Anwar 1988). The Pakistani regime of Zia ul-Haq was opposed to leftists next door, and supported the Mujahideen armed uprising. In December 1979 the Soviet army intervened. Amin was killed and succeeded by Babrak Karmal, who initiated what is called "the second phase."

In 1980 the PDPA slowed down its reform program and announced its intention to eliminate illiteracy in the cities in seven years and in the provinces in ten. In an interview that year Anahita Ratebzad conceded to errors, "in particular the compulsory education of women," to which she added, "the reactionary elements immediately made use of these mistakes to spread discontent among the population" (N. H. Dupree 1984). Despite the slowing down of reforms (including such concessions as the restoration of Islamic family law),[1] the resistance movement spread, supported by Pakistan, the United States, China, the Islamic Republic of Iran, and Saudi Arabia. But the weak Afghan state was unable to impose its will through an extensive administrative and military apparatus. As a result, the program on land redistribution and women's rights faltered. The government's efforts to raise women's status through legal changes regarding marriage were stymied by patriarchal structures highly resistant to change.

Since the Saur Revolution, the population-at-large has more or less ignored the early decrees, and ten years of civil conflict have not produced propitious conditions for social change. The emphasis on "the woman question" has subsided in favor of a concerted effort at "national reconciliation," which began in January 1987. In the constitution of November 1988, the result of a *loya jirga*, or traditional assembly, PDPA members and activists from the Women's Council tried to retain an article stipulating the equality of women with men. This, however, was opposed by the non-PDPA members of the assembly. A compromise was reached in the form of another article which stated that all Afghan citizens, male and female, have equal rights and obligations before the law.[2]

The Transitional Period: Between Revolution and Reconciliation

Article 38 of the Constitution of the Republic of Afghanistan, ratified in November 1987, stated:

> Citizens of the Republic of Afghanistan, both men and women, have equal rights and duties before the law, irrespective of their national, racial, linguistic, tribal, educational and social status, religion, creed, political conviction, occupation, kinship, wealth, and residence. Designation of any illegal privilege of discrimination against rights and duties of citizens are forbidden.

According to government officials with whom I spoke in February 1989, the above article was a compromise, reached after PDPA members and delegates from the Women's Council failed in their attempts to include an equal rights clause.[3]

Many writers on Afghanistan are loath to discuss the positive aspects of the PDPA state's social program, notably its policy on women's rights. Urban, however, notes that "one genuine achievement of the revolution has been the emancipation of (mainly urban) women." He continues: "There is no doubt that thousands of women are committed to the regime, as their prominent participation in Revolutionary Defense Group militias shows. Eyewitnesses stated that militant militiawomen played a key role in defending the besieged town of Urgun in 1983. Four of the seven militia commanders appointed to the Revolutionary Council in January 1986 were women" (Urban 1988: 209).

Despite concessions made in the area of family law, women continued to be active in formal politics. Women were present in the different ranks of the party and the government, with the exception of the council of ministers. The Loya Jirga included women delegates; in 1989 the parliament had seven female members. In 1989, women in prominent positions included Massouma Esmaty Wardak, president of the Afghan Women's Council; Shafiqeh Razmandeh, vice-president of the Afghan Women's Council; Soraya, director of the Afghan Red Crescent Society; Zahereh Dadmal, director of the Kabul Women's Club; and Dr. Soheila, chief surgeon of the Military Hospital, who also holds the rank of general. The central committee of the PDPA had several women members, including Jamila Palwasha and Ruhafza (alternate member), a working-class grandmother and "model worker" at the Kabul Construction Plant (where she did electrical wiring).

In Kabul in January–February 1989, I saw women employees in all government agencies and social organizations visited. Ariana Airlines employed female as well as male flight attendants. A male employee of the Peace, Solidarity, and Friendship Organization laughingly remarked that he was 37 and male, yet his supervisor was ten years younger and female. There were female radio announcers, and the evening news (whether in Pushtu or Dari) was read by one male and one female announcer. Women technicians as well as reporters were working for radio and television, and for the country's newspapers and magazines. Women workers were present in the binding section of a printing house in Kabul, in the page-setting section of the Higher and Vocational Education press house, at the CREPCA state-run carpet company (where young women wove carpets and received a wage), and at the Kabul Construction Plant (which specialized in housing and prefabricated materials). Like their male counterparts, these women were members of the Central Trade Union. I also saw one woman employee (and several female volunteer soldiers) at Pol-e Charkhi prison; she was assigned to the women's section where she oversaw the six remaining female political prisoners, all charged with terrorist acts. I was told that there are women soldiers and officers in the regular armed forces, as well as in the militia and Women's Self-Defense (Defense of the Revolution) Units. There were women in security, intelligence, and the police agencies, women involved in logistics in the defense ministry, and even women veterinarians (an occupation usually off-limits to women in Islamic countries) and parachutists. In 1989 all female members of the PDPA received military training and arms. These women were prominent at a party rally of some 50,000 held in early February 1989.

Schools were now segregated above the primary level, and girls in middle and secondary schools can only be taught by female teachers—a concession made to the traditionalist elements. In offices and other workplaces, however, there was no segregation. Neither were buses divided into male and female sections.

During the 1980s a number of social organizations boasted considerable female participation and visibility. Apart from the PDPA itself, they included the Council of Trade Unions, the Democratic Youth Organization, the Peace, Solidarity, and Friendship Organization, the Afghan Women's Council, and the Red Crescent Society. Next we will consider one of them, the Afghan Women's Council.

The Afghan Women's Council

The most important organization actively involved in women's rights and betterment is the Afghan Women's Council (AWC), a high-profile social organization which until 1989 was run by Massouma Esmaty Wardak and her staff of eight women.[4] Mrs. Wardak was not a PDPA member, though some of her staff were. She is a graduate of the Academy of Sciences with a degree in sociology and an interest in literature and history. Among her published works is a book entitled *The Position and Role of Afghan Women in Afghan Society: From the Late 18th to the Late 19th Century.* She also wrote the introduction to a book on Mahmud Tarzi.

Both Mrs. Wardak and Ms. Soraya (currently president of the Red Crescent Society and formerly head of the Afghan Women's Council) explained that the council is less political and more social and service-oriented than in the past. The AWC provides social services to women, such as literacy and vocational training in such fields as secretarial work, hairdressing, and sewing (workshops are located in the complex); organizes income-generating activities such as handicraft production (mainly rugs and carpets, as well as sewing); offers assistance to mothers and widows of "martyrs of the Revolution" in the form of pensions and coupons; and provides legal advice, mainly through a network of female lawyers. Some women have "outwork" arrangements with the AWC: "They prefer to work at home; they bring their work to us and we pay them." During two trips to the

Women's Council, I was able to observe dozens of women (many of them veiled) entering the grounds to attend a class or to seek advice.

An example of the kind of cases and causes the AWC takes up is the complaint by twenty-two-year-old Najiba, who has been abandoned by her husband for another woman because she could not give him a child. He has since remarried, but the AWC has taken up Najiba's case for maintenance rights in accordance with the law. According to Najiba: "Earlier a woman like me would have had no prospects. Today I am assured of my rights as an individual, and have also been given a job due to the efforts of the AWC."[5]

Mrs. Wardak told me that the AWC has a membership of 150,000, with branches in all provinces except Wardak and Katawaz. The branches organize traditional festivals that include awards for handicraft pieces, and "peace camps" which provide medical care and distribute garments and relief goods free of charge. The branches also assist women in income-generating activities, such as raising chickens and producing eggs and milk for sale, as well as sewing and craftwork. The work of the AWC is supported by the government, which provides it with a generous budget.[6]

The principal objectives of the AWC, according to its president, are raising women's social consciousness, making them aware of their rights, particularly their right to literacy and work, and improving women's living conditions and professional skills. She stressed equal pay with men and workplace child care as two important achievements. But customs die hard, as evidenced by an ongoing radio and TV campaign against the buying and selling of girls. The AWC is also trying to change the laws on child custody that favor the father and his agnates.

Like the AWC, the Kabul Women's Club is located on spacious grounds and holds literacy classes (two-hour classes are held every day) and vocational training, as well as employment workshops where women weave rugs and carpets, sew uniforms, embroider, and produce handicrafts. The work is entirely salaried, and child care and transportation are provided. Courses on house management, health, hairdressing, and typing are offered free of charge. The Afghan Women's Club also works with the Public Health Ministry on mother-

and-child issues, such as disease prevention, vaccination of children, breastfeeding, and family planning.

During the past ten years, the women's organizations have worked among and mobilized hundreds of thousands of Afghan women. Of particular importance to the AWC has been literacy and education of girls. According to a recent AWC survey, there are 7,133 women in institutions of higher education and 233,000 girls studying in schools. The total number of Afghan female professors and teachers is 190 and 22,000 respectively.

In Kabul I asked many party members and workers of the Afghan Women's Council if women's rights would be sacrificed on the altar of national reconciliation. All were fervent believers in the party's duty to defend the gains made in women's rights, and in the ability of the women's organizations to stand up for women's rights to education and employment. Some women with whom I spoke insisted that the April revolution "was made for women." Among women in the capital, there is considerable hostility toward the Mujahideen, and I was told several times that "the women would not allow" a Mujahideen takeover.

A Brief Digression on the Mujahideen and Women in Peshawar

Unlike liberation, resistance, and guerrilla movements elsewhere, the Afghan Mujahideen do not encourage the active participation of women. In Cuba, Algeria, Vietnam, China, Eritrea, Oman, Iran, Nicaragua, El Salvador, and Palestine, women were/are active in the front lines as well as in social services. Significantly, the Mujahideen do not have female spokespersons. Indeed, women in Peshawar who become too visible or vocal are threatened, and sometimes killed. The group responsible for most of the intimidation of women is the fundamentalist *Hizb-e Islami*, led by Gulbeddin Hekmatyar, who has over the years received substantial military, political, and financial support from the United States, Pakistan, and Saudi Arabia. The educational situation in Peshawar is extremely biased against girls. Some 104,600 boys are enrolled in schools against 7,800 girls. For boys there are 486 primary schools, 161 middle schools, and 4 high schools. For girls there are 76 primary schools, 2 middle schools, and no high schools.[7] A UNICEF study indicated that in the camps there are only 180 Afghan women with a high school education. This is consistent with the highly patriarchal arrangements among the Mujahideen and in Peshawar.

As women become excluded from the production of the means of subsistence, their role in human reproduction becomes exaggerated, fetishized. The control of women's fertility and sexuality becomes a matter of family honor. The honor/shame complex in Peshawar is thus a feature of the extreme privatization of the domestic sphere to which women have been relegated, as well as a legacy of the patriarchal social structure. Reintroducing women into public life and social production would change the definition of women's roles. But given the Mujahideen's record on female education, and considering the antipathy toward women's advancement evinced by religious and traditionalist elements, there is no guarantee that, in a post-civil war situation, resources intended for education would be allocated in a gender-equitable fashion. In all likelihood, and in the absence of monitoring, boys would continue to be privileged.

The subordinate status of women is apparently decried by some in Peshawar. The Revolutionary Association of Women of Afghanistan (RAWA) was founded in 1977 (as a Maoist group) but made prominent on 4 February 1987, when its founder, Mina Kishwar Kamal, was killed by fundamentalists in Quetta. RAWA staged a demonstration by women and children in Rawalpindi on 27 December 1988, on the occasion of the ninth anniversary of the Soviet military intervention in Afghanistan. The demonstrators distributed pamphlets attacking in the strongest terms the KGB, Khad (the Afghan secret police), and the Hizb-e Islami. They claimed that the majority of Afghans stood for an independent and democratic Afghanistan, where social justice and freedom to women was guaranteed (Yusufzai 1989). In a communiqué distributed that day, RAWA deplored "the reactionary fanatics [who] are savagely suppressing our grieved people, specially [sic] the women." It continued:

> Killing the innocent men and women, raping, to marry forcefully young girls and widows, and hostility toward women literacy and education, are some customary cruelties committed by the fundamentalists who have

made the life inside and outside the country bitter and suffocating. In their cheap opinion, the women struggle for any right and freedom is regarded as infidelity which must be suppressed brutaly [sic].

The communiqué decried the "antidemocratic and antiwoman" activities of the fundamentalists and warned of "fundamentalist fascism" replacing the current regime.

Summary and Conclusion

At this writing (1991), fundamentalist fascism has not taken over Afghanistan. The Mujahideen have not succeeded in overthrowing the government. However, there has been a marked shift in the government's ideological and programmatic orientation. Following its congress in Spring 1990, the PDPA changed its name to the *Hizb-e Watan*, or the National Party. Constitutional changes were also made, stressing Islam and nation and dropping altogether references to the equality of men and women. The emancipation of women will have to await peace, stability, reconstruction, and development.

This chapter has underscored the importance of the issue of women's rights in the Afghan revolution and civil conflict. It has also explained the subordinate position of women, the resistance to women's rights (including education), and the weak state's inability to implement its reform program in the face of a persistent patriarchy. While Afghanistan is not the only patriarchal country in the world, it is an extreme case of "classic patriarchy." Its rugged terrain and armed tribes have made modernization and centralization a difficult, prolonged, and limited enterprise. This has had serious, and dire, implications for the advancement of women.

Throughout the Third World, women are devising strategies for empowerment and emancipation. In addition to struggling around issues of control over production and reproduction, women have been actively and creatively involved in human rights movements, peace movements, anti-imperialist movements, and movements for social change and equity. One of the most interesting and dynamic examples of a Third World women's movement is that of India, which is strongly anticapitalist and antipatriarchal (Calman 1989; Caplan 1985). It was initiated by women intellectuals and academics concerned about violence against women, and is now constituted by women of the popular classes. It could be an appropriate model for Afghan women. Afghanistan has no mass women's movement and never did, although it has many dedicated women intellectuals, activists, and party cadre who are willing to help initiate one. Perhaps in the near future a popular and autonomous women's movement may emerge, especially as women redefine their roles and assume positions for themselves in the protracted process of reconstruction and development. The Afghan Women's Council and its associated groups should play a significant role in raising women's awareness of their rights, providing women with vital information and services, and organizing and mobilizing women at different levels and sectors of society.

Notes

1. The formal reinstatement of Muslim family law did not apply to party members. Interview with a PDPA official, New York, 28 October 1986.
2. Interview with Farid Mazdak, PDPA official, Kabul, 9 February 1989.
3. Ibid.
4. In 1990 Mrs. Wardak was made minister of education.
5. *Afghanistan Today*, no. 5 (September–October 1988): 22.
6. Interview with Mrs. Esmaty Wardak, 24 January 1989, Kabul.
7. *New York Times*, 2 April 1988, p. A2.

Bibliography

Abu-Lughod, Lila. 1986. *Veiled Sentiments: Honor and Poetry in a Bedouin Society*. Berkeley: University of California Press.
Afghanistan Today (Kabul). Various issues.
Afshar, Haleh, ed. 1985. *Women, Work and Ideology in the Third World*. London: Tavistock.
Anwar, Raja. 1988. *The Tragedy of Afghanistan*. London: Verso.
Boesen, Inger. 1983. "Conflicts of Solidarity in Pukhtun Women's Lives." In *Women in Islamic Society*, ed. Bo Utas. Copenhagen: Scandinavian Institute of Asian Studies, pp. 104–25.
Bourdieu, Pierre. 1965. "The Sentiment of Honor in Kabyle Society." In *Honor and Shame*, ed. J. G. Peristiany. Chicago: University of Chicago Press, pp. 193–241.

Bradsher, Henry. 1985. *Afghanistan and the Soviet Union.* Durham, N.C.: Duke University Press.

Calman, Leslie J. 1989. "Women and Movement Politics in India. *Asian Survey* 29, no. 10 (October):940–58.

Canfield, Robert. 1989. "Afghanistan: The Trajectory of Internal Alignments." *Middle East Journal* 42, no. 4 (Autumn): 635–48.

Caplan, Ann Patricia. 1985. *Class and Gender in India.* London and New York: Tavistock.

Dupree, Louis. 1980. *Afghanistan.* Princeton, N.J.: Princeton University Press.

Dupree, Nancy Hatch. 1984. "Revolutionary Rhetoric and Afghan Women." In *Rebellions and Revolutions in Afghanistan,* ed. Nazif Shahrani and Robert Canfield. Berkeley: University of California, Institute of International Studies.

Ghoussoub, Mai. 1987. "Feminism—or the Eternal Masculine—in the Arab World." *New Left Review* 161 (January–February).

Gregorian, Vartan. 1969. *The Emergence of Modern Afghanistan.* Stanford: Stanford University Press.

Griffiths, John C. 1967. *Afghanistan.* New York: Praeger.

———. 1981. *Afghanistan.* Boulder, Colo.: Westview.

Hammond, Thomas. 1984. *Red Flag over Afghanistan.* Boulder, Colo.: Westview.

Howard-Merriam, Kathleen. 1987. "Afghan Refugee Women and Their Struggle for Survival." In *Afghan Resistance: The Politics of Survival,* ed. Grant Farr and John Merriam. Boulder, Colo.: Westview.

Kabeer, Naila. 1988. "Subordination and Struggle: Women in Bangladesh." *New Left Review* 168 (March/April).

Kandiyoti, Deniz. 1988. "Bargaining with Patriarchy." *Gender and Society* (September).

Katsikas, Suzanne Jolicoeur. 1982. *The Arc of Socialist Revolutions: Angola to Afghanistan.* Cambridge, Mass.: Schenkman Publishing Co.

Keddie, Nikki R. 1989. "The Past and Present of Women in the Muslim World." *Journal of World History* 1, no. 1.

Knauss, Peter. 1987. *The Persistence of Patriarchy: Class, Gender and Ideology in Twentieth-Century Algeria.* Boulder, Colo.: Westview Press.

Lajoinie, Simone Bailleau. 1980. *Conditions de femmes en Afghanistan.* Paris: Notre Temps/Monde.

Lerner, Gerda. 1986. *The Creation of Patriarchy.* Oxford.

Levi-Strauss, Claude. 1969. *The Elementary Structures of Kinship.* Boston: Beacon Press.

Magnus, Ralph H. 1988. "The PDPA Regime in Afghanistan: A Soviet Model for the Future of the Middle East." In *Ideology and Power in the Middle East,* ed. Peter Chelkowski and Robert Pranger. Durham and London: Duke University Press.

Male, Beverly. 1982. *Revolutionary Afghanistan.* New York: St. Martins.

Minces, Juliette. 1982. *The House of Obedience.* London: Zed Books.

Moghadam, V. M. 1990. "Revolution, Culture and Gender: Notes on the Woman Question in Revolution." Paper presented at the Berkshire Conference on the History of Women, Rutgers University (June).

———. 1991. "Revolution, Islam, Women: Sexual Politics in Iran and Afghanistan." Forthcoming in *Nationalisms and Sexualities,* ed. Andrew Ross et al. London and New York: Routledge.

Nyrop, Richard, and Donald Seekins, eds. 1986. *Afghanistan: A Country Study.* Washington, D.C.: The American University, Foreign Area Studies.

Papanek, Hanna. 1985. "Class and Gender in Education-Employment Linkages." *Comparative Education Review* 29, no. 3.

———. 1989. "Socialization for Inequality: Entitlements, the Value of Women, and Domestic Hierarchies." Boston: Center for Asian Development Studies, Boston University.

Revolutionary Association of the Women of Afghanistan. 1988. "Communiqué." Peshawar (December 27).

Roy, Oliver. 1986. *Islam and Resistance in Afghanistan.* Cambridge: Cambridge University Press.

Rubin, Gayle. 1976. "The Traffic in Women: Notes on a Political Economy of Sex." In *Toward an Anthropology of Women,* ed. Rayna Rapp. New York: Monthly Review Press.

Sabbah, Fatna. 1984. *Woman in the Muslim Unconscious.* New York: Pergamon Press.

Stacey, Judith. 1983. *Patriarchy and Socialist Revolution in China.* Berkeley: University of California Press.

Tapper, Nancy. 1984. "Causes and Consequences of the Abolition of Brideprice in Afghanistan." In *Rebellions and Revolutions in Afghanistan,* ed. Nazif Shahrani and Robert Canfield. Berkeley: University of California International Studies Institute, pp. 291–305.

Tillion, Germaine. 1983. *The Republic of Cousins,* trans. Quentin Hoare. London: al-Saqi.

Urban, Mark. 1988. *War in Afghanistan.* New York: St. Martins.

Utas, Bo, ed. 1983. *Women in Islamic Society.* Copenhagen: Scandinavian Institute of Asian Studies.

Wood, Ellen Meiksins. 1988. "Capitalism and Human Emancipation." *New Left Review* 167 (January–February).

Yusufzai, Rahimullah. 1989. "Afghanistan: Withdrawal Symptoms." *The Herald* (January).

Yuval-Davis, Nira, and Floya Anthias, eds. 1989. *Woman-Nation-State.* London: Macmillan.

8

Jewish Fundamentalism

ARTHUR HERTZBERG

The discussion of fundamentalism begins, all too often, with the simplistic notion that literal believers in the sacred scriptures of their faith are political activists. Some are, and some are not. Such division is clearly present among Jewish fundamentalists in their relationship to the major new political fact of Jewish history in the twentieth century, the creation of the State of Israel. One group continues to believe that human effort to restore the Jews to the Holy Land, especially under the aegis of secular nationalists, is a rebellion against the will of God. They are, indeed, "active" in politics, but their activism is the effort to avoid any show of allegiance to the State of Israel. A newer group of fundamentalists accepts the existence of the State of Israel. They regard its creation as a stage in the great, divinely ordained drama of the redemption of the Jewish people from exile.

Such religious and political figures are entirely different from the older fundamentalists. The two groups are divided by more than argument about the correct interpretation of certain texts in Scripture. The older fundamentalists believe that politics belongs permanently to the Gentiles; the newer fundamentalists are "armed prophets," fighting the war of the Lord in this immediate world of politics and power.

The ideological split between passive and activist fundamentalists appeared at the very beginnings of modern Zionism, during the first stirrings in the 1830s toward a revival of the Jewish nation in the Holy Land. Two rabbis, Yehudah Alkalai and Zvi Hirsh Kalisher, reacted to nationalism all around them, in Greece, Hungary, and Germany, by suggesting that the time had come for the oldest of all nations—their own—to return to the Promised Land. Both of these rabbis knew very well the Talmudic texts in which the Jewish people had supposedly promised God Himself that they would not rebel against His decree, to send them into exile, by "ascending [to the Land] as a wall." Jews would not simply try to return en masse; they would wait for the grace of God. This basic promise of fundamentalist passivity had to be finessed, and Alkalai and Kalisher found a way, in the Kabbalah. They quoted the assertion of the mystics that God Himself can be moved by "stirrings below" to act in ways that He had not intended, or, at very least, to move quickly toward goals—such as the redemption of the Jewish people—which He had promised for the unknowable future. These "stirrings below" would move heaven; they would represent the "beginning of the redemption," which God would complete.

Alkalai and Kalisher were the progenitors of "religious Zionism." They made it possible for some Orthodox believers to join with unbelievers to redeem the Land. The overwhelming majority of old believers in the nineteenth and into the twentieth century rejected Zionism, and all of modernity. The Enlightenment and the revolutions in America and France, and eventually in almost all of Europe, were irrelevant, as irrelevant as the appearance of Christianity and the fall of the Roman Empire had been in previous centuries. The basic history of the Jews, so these fundamentalists believed, revolved about only two themes, exile and redemption, and both had been ordained by God. The basic relations of Jews were not with the powers, or movements, of this world.

The fundamentalists had split in the eighteenth century between the Hassidim, who were adherents of charismatic leaders, and the Mitnagdim, who asserted that the essence of Judaism was obedience to the Law. But there was very little difference between these two contending groups in their reaction to Zionist endeavors. To this day, the majority of the Hassidim and the Mitnagdim refuse to recognize the State of Israel. The secular nationalists, who continue to be the major force in Israel, are beyond the pale, but so are the "armed prophets." Indeed, in theory and even, most often, in political practice, the older fundamentalists find it easier to deal with the secular Zionists than with the "armed prophets." Not all of the secular Zionists insist that the State of Israel is the ultimate realization of Judaism, or of the meaning of Jewish history. Some (such as the late Gershom Scholem) hold the view that the creation of Israel was a necessary, rational solution to the needs of Jews in the nineteenth and twentieth centuries, but that this political effort was no substitute for the messianic, redemptive drama. Some of the older fundamentalists can, de facto, come to terms with such Zionists, but the "armed prophets" were, and are, essentially more troublesome. They have asserted that they know what time it was on the clock of redemption. Even worse, they insisted that the Zionist effort, at least in their version, is realizing the redemption, soon.

The battle between the fundamentalists and the "religious Zionists"—the spiritual descendants of Alkalai and Kalisher, was waged in various forms for very nearly a century. At first, the ideological issue was of secondary importance, for neither group of fundamentalists—not even the "religious Zionists"—believed that the redemption was imminent. Never mind that Theodore Herzl had confided to his diary in 1897, at the opening of the first World Zionist Congress, the prediction that there would be a Jewish state in fifty years. Most Zionists were not that boldly visionary. Therefore many secularists waited for the gradual conquest of the Land, "one cow and one dunam" at a time; others thought that historic cataclysms such as the First World War provided opportunities for revolutionary and transforming political acts. The "religious Zionists" were thus free to believe that at some unspecified moment, as men and women built settlements, God would intervene—but not just yet.

A new, transforming—and ultimately threatening—motif was introduced in the first two decades of the twentieth century by Rabbi Abraham Isaac Kook. He would become, in 1921, the first chief rabbi of the Jewish community in Palestine as it was formally constituted by the Zionists under the British Mandate. Kook was a religious revolutionary who believed that the time of redemption had already begun. The First World War, so he wrote in the very midst of it, was proof of the suicidal bankruptcy of the Christian West. The time was at hand when the Jews would resume their ordained function of leading the world to live in the sight of God. The Zionist return to the land of Israel was the first act of the redemptive drama which would soon, in our day, climax with all the glories that had been foretold about the coming of the Messiah.

Abraham Isaac Kook was a gentle man. He sounded no call to arms, because that was against his temperament, and against the prevailing atmosphere in the Zionist movement as a whole. The dominant ideology among secular Zionists was humanistic social-ism, which believed that the dream of national rebirth in the land would be achieved by building the new Jewish society. Jews thought of themselves, then, as defending their settlements in Palestine against Arab attack and not as conquerors of the land by force. But Kook was not merely reflecting the dominant mood of the moment. He was famous for his warm feelings toward even antireligious Zion-ists, the rebels against God who were creating the Kibbutzim and helping to revive the Hebrew language as a modern, secular tongue. But Kook was so accepting because he saw these "heretics" as un-witting instruments in the hand of God. He knew, as they did not, that they were really acting out some of the preparation for the coming of the Messiah. Reclaiming the land and reviving the lan-guage were sacred acts, the very sacredness of which would ulti-mately bend those who perform them to the will of God. As the Catholic writer Graham Greene once said, "God was writing straight through crooked lines." Kook knew what God was writing, and what time it was on His clock.

Kook's revolutionary idea, that he had perceived the divine inten-tion in contemporary political acts, was a genie being let out of the bottle. Like all genies, it would be uncontrollable. If some political acts, such as building secular kibbutzim in the midst of hostile Arabs, were part of God's plan, it is at least conceivable that other acts, such as failing to defend an exposed kibbutz and abandoning it to Arabs, were against God's will. A secular authority—a Zionist central body or a Jewish state, not to speak of some Gentile power—

which might ordain such action could be defined as illegitimate. To oppose such decisions is not unlawful or even treasonable. On the contrary, it is the truest obedience to which man can be called. The gentle mystic can thus be transformed, at least by some of his followers, into a defiant armed prophet, which is exactly what happened to Abraham Isaac Kook. His son, Zvi Yehudah, eventually succeeded him as head of the *yeshivah* which the father had founded. The young men trained in this school affirmed their Zionism by serving in Israel's army, as the older, passivist fundamentalists would not. More and more the disciples of Zvi Yehudah Kook moved from training priests for future service in the Holy Temple to longing for, and being eager to fight for, the restoration of all of the Land of Israel to Jewish hands. Even before the Six-Day War in June 1967, Zvi Yehudah Kook exhorted his followers toward action in regaining Judea and Samaria. The very earth of these regions was longing, he asserted, to reencounter the Jews, the rightful inhabitants to whom God had promised all of the Holy Land. The victory in the Six-Day War was immediately understood by Kook, the younger, and by his followers as proof that the age of redemption had indeed arrived. All of the land was now in Jewish hands, and it was now necessary only to ensure that all of it was made inalienable. The "armed prophets" split into factions, but the movements to settle Judea and Samaria, the radicals who wanted to expel the Arabs, and those who plotted to dynamite the Muslim shrines on the Temple Mount were all nourished from the same source: the teaching that the days of the Messiah were at hand, and that those who stood in the way of his coming should be removed or pushed aside.

In recent years, detailed accounts of the actions of the various factions among "armed prophets" have appeared with increasing frequency in a number of languages, especially in Hebrew and English. This essay is not an attempt at such a history but rather at an analysis of the underlying theological structure of the two major varieties of Jewish fundamentalism. From the perspective of the older, anti-Zionist fundamentalists, the new "armed prophets" are heretics. They are regularly denounced in the publications of the older group as reevoking the most dangerous of all the false messiahs, Shabtai Zvi, who appeared in the Eastern Mediterranean region in the middle of the seventeenth century. Zvi had announced that he knew the year of the redemption, 1666, and that, amidst divine miracles, he would lead the scattered Jewish people back to the land. Today's "armed prophets" are often called contemporary Shabtai Zvis by their religious critics.

For theoretical purposes, one question remains: Whom do the "armed prophets" represent? Do they come of a different socioeconomic class than the passivist fundamentalists, or than the rest of Jewish society in Israel or the Diaspora? Many analysts have maintained that revived Islamic fundamentalism represents the *suk*, the petty bourgeois who feel dispossessed in modern, technological society. Such class analysis simply does not work when applied to Jewish fundamentalism. In all its varieties, the camp of the "armed prophets" is no different in social composition than the rest of Israel. Indeed, the members of Gush Emunim and the "faithful" of the Temple Mount are as well educated, and as middle class as most Ashkenazi Israelis. The difference is ideological; it is a matter of belief and not an expression of class anger.

One must beware of equating the "armed prophets" with a much larger constituency in Israel that advocates toughness toward the Arabs. It is true that the majority of those who adhere to the hard line are poor Sephardim. It is they who hail General Sharon as "Arik, King of the Jews." Here class anger at the Ashkenazim, who long dominated the Israeli establishment, is indeed being expressed, along with many centuries of remembered hurt at the hands of the Arab majority in the North African lands from which most Sephardim emigrated. This political constituency, which is now the core of the Likud vote, is not to be equated with fundamentalists, old or new. Some of their religious leaders do belong to the "armed prophets," but their greatest spiritual authorities definitely do not. The most authoritative of all voices is that of Rabbi Ovadaih Yosef, who was once the Sephardi Chief Rabbi of Israel. He continues to insist, and to instruct his political followers, that the time of the redemption is God's own secret, and that, in the here and now, it would be permissible for an Israeli government to return land in Judea and Samaria to Arab rule, if that would save lives. In Israel, the *shuq* does harbor class anger, and it votes for Ashkenazi leaders who are populists, but

Shamir and even Sharon are secular nationalists and not religious fundamentalists. A populist leadership that was dovish could conceivably lead these elements in a different direction.

The "armed prophets" of Israel, and their supporters throughout the Jewish world, are a very nearly pure example of ideology in politics.

9

Jewish Zealots:
Conservative versus Innovative

MENACHEM FRIEDMAN

When zealot groups in Israel are discussed, two diametrically opposed religious-political viewpoints—Neturei Karta (NK) and Gush
Emunim (GE)—are considered the two poles on Israel's religious
map. In this chapter, these groups are shown to be manifestations of
two types of fundamentalism: "conservative" in the case of NK, and
"innovative" (or revolutionary) in the case of GE.

Because the concept of fundamentalism originally evolved within
the framework of the history of Christianity,[1] the term cannot always
be used in the same way with reference to non-Christian religions,
such as Judaism or Islam. We use the term to define a religious
outlook shared by a group of believers who base their belief on an
ideal religious-political reality that has existed in the past or is expected to emerge in the future. Such realities are described in great
detail in the religious literature. And the fundamentalist believer is
obliged to use whatever religious and political means are necessary
to actualize these realities in the here and now.

Both conservative and innovative fundamentalism refer to the traditional Jewish religious conception of Jewish history, which is said to
be in a state of dialectical tension between "Exile" and "Redemption."
However, although redemption signifies an ideal religious-political
reality, paradoxically, within contemporary Orthodox Jewish society,

the exilic past—particularly that which evolved in Eastern Europe—
is viewed nostalgically as the very model of Jewish life. Thus, conservative fundamentalism looks to the past; any deviation from the
idealized Jewish society, whether on the religious-social or religious-
political plane, must be fought. From this perspective conservative
fundamentalists condemn as "deviant" the Jewish reality in the State
of Israel today.

Radical or innovative fundamentalism, on the other hand, sees a
diametrically opposite "reality," one in which the State of Israel
today exists in a condition that is categorically different from the
exilic state. Although radical fundamentalists do not view the reality
of the State of Israel today as a sign of complete redemption, they do
perceive it as a signal that the period of the "footsteps of the Messiah"
is beginning. Thus, images and precepts that are part of the traditional messianic literature sometimes assume radical "new" significance for innovative fundamentalists.

Although Neturei Karta ("Guardians of the City") cannot really
be regarded as a formally organized movement,[2] more attempts
than ever before are currently being made to organize in an in-
stitutionalized framework those who identify with its religious-
ideological views. These attempts have been increased since the
deaths of two NK founders and leaders, Amram Blau and Aharon
Katzenelbogen.[3] By virtue of their personalities and work, they succeeded in spontaneously rallying many of those who had identified
with the entire NK ideology and practices or had joined the group
because they agreed with one or more of the issues it was fighting for.
The deaths of Blau and Katzenelbogen created a vacuum that exacer-
bated existing differences and tensions between NK—which represents the extreme isolationist view that rejects every form of contact
with the political-economic Zionist establishment—and the Edah
Haredit,[4] another ultra-Orthodox group that rejects the aspirations of
Zionism in Palestine by adhering to the principle of "isolationism."

The increased tensions arose because, as an organized community,
the Edah has been forced to compromise with the political-economic
reality of the State of Israel in order to ensure that its members
receive the full complex of communal services. This is in contrast
with NK which, despite attempts to become more structured, re-

mains a fairly loose, mostly spontaneous association of people who define themselves as "zealots" in the terminology of traditional Judaism. Whereas the NK to a certain degree is a protest group, its zealotry goes much further than mere protest. Deeply rooted in the Jewish religion, zealotry expresses the tension between a religion based on ancient sacred writings and the reality that characterizes the Jewish religion in today's world.

Neturei Karta first appeared in the wake of the political developments of the 1930s, when the conflict between the Jewish *yishuv* and militant Arab nationalism was becoming increasingly violent and the Nazis were rising to power in Germany. These developments impelled Agudat Israel,[5] the extreme anti-Zionist Jewish religious-political movement that until then had included NK leaders, to reconcile itself to some forms of political cooperation with the Zionist leadership in Palestine. This signified a major turning point for Agudat Israel, which had opposed Zionist *yishuv* institutions from the beginning of the British mandate, when the Agudah and the Edah were identical in Palestine. Agudah-Edah activities aimed at delegitimizing Zionist efforts to establish a new secular Jewish society in *Eretz Israel* found their most stringent expression in the "exodus" of both from the organized Zionist communities (*knesset Israel*) and in the establishment of the Edah as an anti-Zionist group on its own. But, after the riots of 1929 in Palestine and the worsening economic and political position of Jews in Poland and Germany, Agudat Israel saw no choice but to identify with the minimum demands of the Zionist *yishuv*, in order to ensure Jewish immigration, especially for its own members.

The problems of European Jewry notwithstanding, Amram Blau and Aharon Katzenelbogen, who were then the leaders of Tzeirei ("The Young Guard") Agudat Israel, remonstrated against the Agudah for having betrayed its fundamental principles in abandoning isolation by cooperating with secular Zionist organizations and institutions. Originally calling themselves Ha-Chaim ("Life"), they adopted the Aramaic name Neturei Karta ("Guardians of the City") in 1939, when Blau and his circle published a proclamation against a fundraising campaign—in actuality a tax—for defending Jews against the Arab revolt of 1936–39. The name derives from a passage in the Jerusalem Talmud (Hagiga 76:B) that calls religious scholars rather than armed watchmen the guardians and true defenders of the city. In its proclamation the group argued that, as religious students and scholars, they (NK), and not the defense units of the Zionists (Haganah), were the guardians of the city, as the latter desecrated the Sabbath in public and did not observe the dietary laws of *kashrut*, in line with the secular character of Zionism. Amram Blau and his friends raised this challenge both verbally and in writing. They even raised it physically, when they took to the streets to interfere with attempts to collect the "defense" money.

Although secular Zionists were the proclaimed enemy, Agudat Israel became the principal target of the NK protest. For, in the eyes of NK, the Agudah was unwittingly helping to legitimize the Zionist organization by cooperating with this effort. When Edah Haredit elections were held in July 1945, NK, in cooperation with some Edah leaders, obtained control over its institutions and ousted the representatives of Agudat Israel from this body.

Although NK and the Edah expressed the same political-religious point of view after July 1945, they still differed in organization and function. The Edah was and still is a communal organization with its own bureaucracy, whose main function is to provide its members with communal services, in particular with regard to *kashrut* and personal status (marriage and divorce). Yet, paradoxically, the very same isolationist principle that dictates providing separate religious and communal services has forced the Edah to accommodate itself to "Zionist-atheist" institutions in order to have the wherewithal to do so.

After the State of Israel was established in 1948, political reality as well as financial need dictated some form of cooperation with the state. For example, even the most extreme and anti-Zionist elements are not prepared to relinquish government sanction of marriages, as without it the Edah could not take any binding legal measures against a member who leaves his wife and children. Although some protracted and enervating procedures for applying pressure are always available in such a community, the outcome is not at all certain. They therefore must accept formal authorization from the Ministry of Religious Affairs in order to perform legally binding marriages and to grant divorces. Further, the provision of separate Edah *kashrut* services necessitates municipal and sometimes also governmental licenses (e.g., for slaughtering houses), as well as arrangements with Zionist enterprises and corporations such as Tnuvah (a Histadrut affiliate), which supplies most of the country's dairy products, fruit, and vegetables. Moreover, having its own bureaucracy has almost inevitably led the Edah to make further concessions in its isolationist principle when it fights for its economic interests by trying to gain a greater share of the Israeli food market for ultra-kosher products. As long as the standard of living in Israel remained low, these tendencies were hardly noticeable. But by the mid-1960s, as it rose and the *haredi* (ultra-Orthodox), community sought to share in it, an increasingly sharp controversy developed between NK and Edah leaders.

The controversies between NK and the Edah, between these two and Agudat Israel, and between all three and secular Jewish society provide the background and context for the activities of radical extremist elements in NK and related groups, whose acts of religious zeal often take on a verbal and physical violence. Paradoxical as it may seem, these activities are directed not only against the secular Zionist but also against recognized, accepted rabbinic authorities and distinguished leaders of the ultra-Orthodox groups. Again paradoxically, these expressions of the tension between groups are based on shared historiosophical and historiographical views as *yahadut haredit: haredi* Jewry. It is only with this knowledge that we can understand such acts of religious zeal and their dialectical nature, for it is my thesis that this particular social context fosters conservative fundamentalism.

Without elaborating on the development of the term *yahadut haredit*, the historiosophical and historiographical principles that determine the social confinement of this society are formulated in a brief and in a somewhat simplified manner.

1. The term "Jewish nation" is meaningful only within the context of the mystical unity of Israel, the Torah, and God. Thus, Jewish identity has meaning only when there is faith in God, as well as in the Torah (both written and oral) as the expression of His absolute

will. The Torah must therefore be obeyed by observing the halakhic commandments as interpreted by the *gedolei ha-Torah* (Torah sages) of every generation.

2. The historic destiny of the Jewish people derives from the special relationship between the Jewish nation and God, as described in the biblical quote, "Not like the other nations is the house of Israel." The Jewish nation cannot escape its special historic destiny of exile and redemption, both of which are basic concepts of Jewish existence. Agudat Israel, Edah Haredit, and NK all define Jewish existence in the current political reality of Zionism and the State of Israel as being in a state of exile; whereas the adherents of Zionism define it as "the return of the Jewish people to history," and ultra-Orthodox Jews view it as a revolt against the "not [being] like other nations." The *haredi* viewpoint, perforce, views Zionist attempts to control Jewish history as a mutiny against God. This viewpoint leads to its isolationist principle and policy toward Zionist institutions and the State of Israel. Hence, every deviation from this policy, if justified at all, is justified on pragmatic grounds alone, in other words, *a posteriori.*

3. The way of life that developed in traditional Jewish communities, especially in the Ashkenazi communities of Central and Eastern Europe before the process of modernization and secularization (*haskalah*) began, is viewed as the fullest expression of Jewish society. Thus, *haredi* ultra-Orthodoxy takes this traditional Jewish society as its standard for determining the legitimacy of Orthodox Jewish life in the modern reality. From this point of view, *haredi* ultra-Orthodox religiosity to a large extent can be defined as "neo-traditionalism," a term used here deliberately because *haredi* religiosity is certainly not consistent with traditional religiosity. Although one finds traditional religionists, whose adherence to the traditional way of life is absolute and who make no attempt whatsoever to adjust to modern society, *haredi* Jews seem to be able to deviate from tradition when necessary. However, it should again be stressed that any changes in traditional ways of life are justified only *a posteriori*, generally as a concession to social or personal imperfection.

Haredi society therefore is viewed hierarchically, in accordance with the degree of adherence to the old way of life. Since adherence to tradition as expressed in outer appearance (traditional garments, beard, side-locks), speech (Yiddish), and the education of children (*heder*) is considered the most legitimate, Neturei Karta who follow the traditions of the Old Ashkenazi *yishuv* in these respects are not merely the best representative of the isolationist approach, but also the embodiment of extreme and uncompromising loyalty to the traditions of "Israel of old."[6]

Haredi self-identification therefore is determined not only by its special historiosophical and historiographical points of view but also by the awareness of the degree to which these have been deviated from on the political, religious, and social levels. Thus, *haredi* society is characterized by continuous feelings of self-delegitimation, guilt, and weakness *a posteriori* in the face of Zionist reality. These feelings determine the strength of NK as a radical religious group. To a large extent they also determine its dialectical relation with all of *haredi* ultra-Orthodoxy, as well as, in a sense, with religious Jewish society in general.

But radical though they may be, these paradoxical and complicated relations place NK and similar groups in the camp of conservative fundamentalism. This is because Jewish traditional society is their context of reference and they consider themselves living in conditions of exile, which limits their use of power to traditional "exilic" means of behavior. Religious groups such as NK express their radical viewpoints in activities that they call *zealotism*, viewing this as a legitimate religious phenomenon in the context of Judaism. The classical example of such religious zeal is that of Pinhas, son of Elazar, son of Aaron the Priest, who killed both Zimri, son of Salu, "a chief in the Simeonite family," and Cozbi the Midianite, daughter of Zur, before the entire congregation of the children of Israel.[7] The Talmudic commentary on this event provides the following sociological analysis of Pinhas' act.[8] Although God praises Pinhas in the Bible, the Talmud justifies his deed only *a posteriori*. The ambivalent attitude toward such direct, violent acts may be sensed in the discussion between the Talmud sages. The Talmud says that if Zimri had killed Pinhas, he would not have been punished, "for he [Pinhas] is a persecutor." And when a man chases his fellow with a weapon in his hand, he who takes the life of the pursuer does not have to be punished, as he has in fact saved the lives of those being pursued. However, a deed such as that of Pinhas can be justified only "if it was committed spontaneously, in a mood of uncontrollable anger."

Despite the ambivalence of the halakhic sages, they recognize that such outbursts are inevitable expressions of religious emotion. But, as it is described in the Talmud,[9] the story reflects another important aspect of the "zeal syndrome": the tension between zealots and their leaders. For, by acting in front of the entire congregation, Pinhas demonstrated the weakness of the leader Moses. Indeed, it is one of the crucial aspects of this syndrome that, whatever their intention, zealots always end up challenging the established religious leadership. Even though their anger is directed at sinners, it ultimately implies criticism of the established leaders, however respected they may otherwise be.

Numerous examples of religious zeal, manifested in acts of verbal and physical violence against "sinners," can be found in various historical contexts. However, such acts are more likely to occur during periods characterized by secularization, when religion has lost control over the behavior of the people. For example, the old Ashkenazi *yishuv* in Jewish Jerusalem at the turn of the century provided a particularly favorable climate for religious zealots. The process of change and modernization that took place in Jerusalem toward the end of the nineteenth century, triggered by the activity of Western European Jewish philanthropic organizations with reformist tendencies, made possible the development of an economically and socially strong class of intellectuals (*maskilim*). But, although this new way of life was regarded as antithetical to the tradition of the old *yishuv*, the religious leadership was too weak to take serious action against it. The difficult economic and political situation also compelled them to rely upon these deviators from tradition to maintain contact between them and the philanthropic organizations. However, precisely this weakness of the religious leadership allowed the zealots relative freedom of action.

Within the social structure of the old *yishuv*, among rabbis who possessed authority and were respected in the traditional Jewish world, the zealots were able to find religious authorities to be their patrons and to sanction their activities. From this point of view, such figures as Rabbis Y. L. Diskin and J. H. Sonnenfeld played a very important role in the phenomenon of religious zeal in Jerusalem. This patronage also had economic significance. For the rabbinic scholars who sanctioned the activities of the zealots enabled them to assume a relatively independent position in the economic set-up and power centers of their society by supporting them while they devoted their time to religious activities. Thus, the tradition of religious zeal that developed in Jerusalem constituted a source of direct or indirect subsistence by allowing zealotism to become a "profession." And this structure has remained the same in essence to this very day.

An analysis of zealot activities demonstrates that they are facilitated by three levels of participation on the part of their community:

1. *Active zealots.* Unlike Pinhas, who acted alone, the zealots' acts of verbal or physical violence usually are influenced by the group. In other words, those who act against either "sinners" or rabbinical authorities—by shouting, protesting, blows, or vilification—usually act as a group, with mutual encouragement.

2. *Sympathizers or passive zealots.* Public sympathy for zealotry is a complex phenomenon. Its sympathizers range from those who support activists wholeheartedly and publicly yet do not dare to join them, to those who object to the acts themselves yet refrain from doing anything that might lead to the identification or arrest of the perpetrators because they identify with their final aims.

3. *Rabbinical patrons.* Recognized and respected rabbinical authorities legitimize zealous acts. They are especially necessary when such acts are directed against other rabbinical authorities.

The relationships among these three groups are neither static nor fixed, but rather dynamic. Nor are they harmonious; indeed, they are subject to permanent tension stemming from the violent and unpremeditated nature of some zealous acts.

Against such a social reality, violence is inherent to acts of religious zeal. Indeed, in the case of Pinhas, the archetypical zealot, the violence led to death. This has not been the case with *haredi* zealots, whose violence is confined mostly to verbal or written harassment and the destruction of property. Although people have been hurt by stones thrown at cars traveling on the Sabbath, this has not resulted in any fatal injury. Moreover, the zealots have never taken up weapons or used any other means deliberately aimed at killing people.

The reasons for this restraint are critical to our understanding of the distinction between conservative and innovative fundamentalism, for one of the factors that leads *haredi* zealots to exhibit restraint is their awareness of mutual Jewish responsibility, which is strengthened by their very affinity to Jewish tradition. However, they express this in a very curious manner: even when they are explicitly stating their hope that the mutinous and atheistic State of Israel will vanish, they add:

> This Lord of the Universe . . . knows how to lead His world in mercy and benevolence and to remove the obstacles and delays of the coming of the Messiah [an allusion to the State of Israel] without, Heaven Forbid, hurting anyone in Israel. . . . He who passed over the houses of Israel in Egypt and saved those who waited for redemption shall also show us wondrous things at the time of future redemption.[10]

This quote, by one of the main supporters of the zealots in Jerusalem, is evidence that, despite all their differences with other Jews, there is a clear sense of a common Jewish fate in a hostile world.

The affinity of extremist zealots for the complex social structure that constitutes Orthodox society in its entirety, and their dependence on it as well as on recognized religious authorities, inevitably keeps their activities within tolerable confines. And, because they do not serve in the army, extremist *haredi* zealots usually are not familiar with the use of firearms. In fact, as a very small and visible minority, they can easily be harmed themselves.

Finally, the extremists have no political ambitions in terms of reaching positions of power within Israeli society. On the contrary, they want to continue to live in exile as a minority protected by the powers that be. The central religious import of the concept of exile in traditional Jewish society is not merely a political-geographical one delineating relations between Jews and the society and sovereign political framework that surround them. It is essentially religious in that it determines the historical framework of Jewish existence as the basis of the unique relationship between the Jewish people and God. According to kabbalistic tradition, notably that of the Lurianic Kabbalah, the reality of exile encompasses the divine system itself, which has been "damaged," as it were, and requires "restoration."

To define the historical reality as one of exile is to evoke much of halakhic significance that does not admit of elaboration within the present framework. Fundamentally, however, defining the political reality as one of exile serves as a mechanism of adaptation to the unique conditions of Jewish existence on both the political and religious-halakhic planes. Therefore, not only are Torah laws relating to or bound up with Temple rites sequestered from day-to-day Jewish life in exile, but the entire network of precepts dealing with relations between Jews and gentiles is perceived as not binding in accordance with the Jew's political experience as a persecuted minority.[11]

Two levels of simultaneously existing religious rulings are discernible within this framework. One bears an affinity to the political reality of exile, and the second relates to a utopian "reality" that either existed in the past or is destined to emerge in the future, when "Israel's hand shall be high." The reality of exile enables political-social ideas from the non-Jewish world to be absorbed and adopted while preserving a binding and fundamental affinity to religious-political precepts that are completely opposed to such ideas. Indeed, ever since the emergence of the modern era, Jewish society has been characterized by the existence of two different worlds, which demand contradictory systems of social-cultural norms.

Without going too deeply into the different interpretations given to exile by various groups of *Halakhah*-bound Orthodox Jewry, some remarks are called for on the Jewish society in *Eretz Israel* as it evolved through the agency of the Zionist movement. Secular in nature, the Zionist movement sought to establish a sovereign Jewish society that would be "modern" not only on the technological plane but also, and perhaps chiefly, on the culture-value plane. In such a democratic society, it was envisioned, non-Jews would enjoy full personal and religious equality, in contrast to the discrimination and persecution that Jews and Jewish culture had suffered in non-Jewish societies. These basic concepts were first put to the test in *Eretz*

Israel in the formative stage of Zionism, when the religious-political question of women's right to vote for institutions of self-government arose after Britain took over Palestine.[12] The two positions of principle adduced on this issue were the modern-secular view, which could not accept discrimination against women as it conflicted with the political-social values of modern society, and the religious outlook, grounded in Halakhah and in the values of the traditional religious society. This question was not resolved in the religious community as a whole, as it split along the lines of Zionist and anti-Zionist identification. The anti-Zionists, who rejected Zionism as an attempt to annul the state of exile by secular-political-material means, viewed the enfranchisement of women as a substantive expression of secular Zionism. As such, they refused to take part in the Jewish institutions established at the outset of British mandatory rule in Palestine.

Notwithstanding halakhic pronouncements by rabbinical authorities whom it also accepted, the religious Zionism that found expression in the stand of the Mizrachi movement[13] relied upon halakhic rulings of other authorities, who acquiesced in the secular Zionists' stand on this question. Although the Mizrachi movement's "decision" on the issue of women's enfranchisement did not follow from its obligation to *Halakhah*, it viewed itself as true to its commitment to both the Jewish people, the Torah, and God, on the one hand, and to the national goals of the Zionist movement, on the other. This is what led to their imbuing the Zionist enterprise in *Eretz Israel* with a "positive" religious definition in terms of the traditional concepts of Exile and Redemption, and of what underlies the fundamentalist religious innovation of religious Zionism. This principle of religious Zionism vis-à-vis exile and redemption, which was concealed and downplayed in the past, is highly visible in the radical religiosity of Gush Emunim's Zionism.

Paradoxically enough, within the framework of the dialectic between exile and redemption, the ability of religious Zionism to cope with the secularization process undergone by Jewish Palestine was almost inevitably grounded in the religious conception of the uniqueness of Jewish history, of being "not like all the other nations." In other words, it was based on a principled religious outlook holding that the historical process, as it evolved in Palestine, implied a change in the state of exile or the transition to the state of redemption. Hence, the "secularization" of the Jewish community in Palestine, as part of a reconstructed sovereign Jewish society, could be perceived and explicated both in terms of the sanctification of the entire historical process and as an essential part of a divine plan for the redemption of Jewish people by extricating them from the state of exile.

These concepts were given their full expression in the writings of Rabbi Abraham Isaac ha-Cohen Kook.[14] Though religious Zionists did not necessarily accept all or even part of Rabbi Kook's religious philosophy, such realities of Jewish existence as World War II and the establishment of the State of Israel as a sovereign political entity were perceived as an inherent part of the process of redemption. In other words, the fact that the State of Israel offered Jews a place for in-gathering from exile was enough to accord religious legitimization to it and even to the secular Jewish society existing there. These same basic principles, however, also became the rationale for another kind of political radicalism and fundamentalist religious positions derived from Jewish "writings" relating to Redemption.

The Six-Day War was a turning point in the political expression of religious radicalism. If Israel's 1948 War of Independence is viewed as a Zionist war for the establishment of an emergent secular Jewish state, the Six-Day War can be defined as a Jewish war that reflected a substantive historical change in dialectic between exile and redemption. For, whereas the Six-Day War did not necessarily constitute total and absolute transition from exile to redemption, it marked the point at which a substantially different religious reality came into existence.

The background to this development stems from social changes in the Israeli polity, as well as from such historical circumstances as Israel's rapid and astonishing victory over Egypt, Jordan, and Syria, which brought all of *Eretz Israel* under Jewish rule. Now that places denoting the Jewish people's essential affinity to *Eretz Israel*—such as Jerusalem with the Temple Mount at its center and Hebron with its Tomb of the Patriarchs—had come under Jewish rule, a new geopolitical reality was created. And the young religious-Zionist elite that encountered this new reality was ready to accord the war and the situation it generated an existential-religious meaning through which the State of Israel became the Land of Israel and the Zionist state the Jewish state. This concatenation of events led to the emergence of Gush Emunim, a movement that regards itself as religious-Zionist in its fulfillment and within whose framework expression has been given to fundamentalist concepts that represent what I term *innovative fundamentalism.*

Religious Zionism represents an attempt to combine a modern way of life with observance of *Halakhah* as it traditionally has been interpreted. The consolidation of modern religiosity inevitably entailed selecting the traditions and practices that conformed to this new way of life. Thus, some traditional elements were excluded and observance of such central Jewish commandments as prayer, Torah study, and premarital chastity became less stringent. The pattern of life that emerged from this basically spontaneous and socially activated process might be termed one of diminished religiosity.[15] Although this religiosity allowed religious Zionist Jews to play a role in the developing society and its economy without affecting their self-identification as Orthodox Jews, there was no ideological development in this atmosphere. Once the intensive pioneering activity of prestate *Eretz Israel* leveled off, and the rise in living standards facilitated the establishment of high-school *yeshivot*, religious Zionist youth became aware of the painful contradiction between their parents' way of life and what they felt was prescribed in the halakhic literature they studied. The helplessness of parents in the face of this direct and indirect criticism from their children began a delegitimation of parents that has had social and political repercussions. Whereas some of the national religious youngsters who graduated from high-school *yeshivot* were absorbed by ultra-Orthodox "great" *yeshivot*, others went on to those that were more in line with the principles of religious Zionism. The oldest and most important of these latter *yeshivot* was the Mercaz ha-Rav Yeshivah of Rabbi A. I. Kook. Under the direction of his son Zvi Yehudah Kook, Mercaz ha-Rav presented young people with a world view that offered a meaningful religious existence in the State of Israel in accordance with Zvi Yehudah's interpretation of his father's teachings.

Rabbi Kook's historiographic views are directly opposed to those of *haredi* ultra-Orthodoxy. His doctrine perceives the historical reality of his generation as more complex and essentially dialectical. In this view, the reality defined as "the footsteps of the Messiah" is considered part of the historical development toward future redemption, because it views secular-Zionist society as playing a positive and crucial role in the messianic process, which is also essentially dialectical in nature.

Although Rabbi Kook's use of the concept "the footsteps of the Messiah" was not intended to express an innovation in religious Zionist policy, it constituted a turning point in Jewish religious thought. Indeed, extremist zealot fears regarding the potential for innovation and change are not without basis, since the concept was meant to help religious Zionism integrate into Zionist society and politics in *Eretz Israel* as a "junior partner." Thus, as a religious-political manifestation, Gush Emunim reflects changes in the religious-Zionist community in *Eretz Israel* on two levels:

1. On the plane of historical consciousness within the framework of the dialectic between exile and redemption, GE reflects an awareness and inner sense of confidence that the "history" of the Jewish people has already passed the incipient stage of the "footsteps of the Messiah"—although it is still not clear exactly how far Jewish history has advanced in the stage of Redemption.

2. In the normative-halakhic sphere, GE essentially signifies the criticism and rejection of "light" religiosity and a concomitant commitment to the strict and stringent religiosity demonstrated, paradoxically enough, by the ultra-Orthodox standardbearers of "anti-Zionist" religiosity: the Haredim.

A comparison of the conservative religious radicalism of *haredi* Neturei Karta and the innovative radicalism manifested by various circles within Gush Emunim reveals many structural similarities. Fundamentally, both forms base themselves on the same "writings" and see themselves as committed to the same halakhic-midrashic-kabbalistic literature. However, as NK unequivocally defines the historical reality as a state of exile, it regards any deviation from the "traditional" way of life as constituting a "revolt" against divine providence. In contrast, by designating the current historical situation a state of redemption, GE broadens the historical frame of reference to encompass the "utopian realities" in traditional religious literature, which lay down different norms, especially in the political-religious sphere.

Indeed, the religious radicalism of Gush Emunim encompasses features that were of only theoretical import in the stage of exile but that suddenly became "compatible" with the new political situation as interpreted by GE's religious leaders. However, in areas relating to "normal," day-to-day life, GE manifests a clear tendency to reject "diminished religiosity" in favor of the "strict religiosity," characteristic of today's Haredim, of which NK is an integral part. However, the "innovative" religious radicalism of Gush Emunim sometimes finds itself in polar conflict with conservative fundamentalism, the differences between them relating to elements central to the Jewish faith—for example, to the question of a Jewish religious presence on the Temple Mount. Moreover, as we have seen, the relations between groups such as Neturei Karta and religious authorities accepted by ultra-Orthodox Jewry place restrictions on their freedom of action as well. For the dialectic that characterizes these relations is an integral part of the self-identity of members of these groups as traditional Jews committed to heeding the instructions of "Torah sages."

The radical-religious groups who feel that the fundamental change after the Six-Day War denotes a new religious-historical experience are bound along a new track from the outset. Their certainty that there is a reality that differs substantively from the traditional one, one that is as experiential as it is imbued in consciousness, must encompass elements of a religious-political activism that will find little if any legitimation in religious authorities outside their own frameworks. Moreover, this certainty, which derives its sanction from the political reality of Jewish control over all of *Eretz Israel*, requires the legitimation of religious authorities who are even more of an anathema to Orthodox Jewry. Yet, it is precisely the gap that inevitably exists within a political reality that is both the very actualization and symbol of extrication from the states of exile and redemption which is expressed in Israel's democratic character. This tension will no doubt become increasingly intolerable as time passes. "Painful" contradictory realities, such as Muslim worship on the Temple Mount, are liable to push groups of individuals into seeking renewed sanction for what they feel is the character and essence of current Jewish history. And the need for repeated sanction of the inner reality of redemption in the face of the more complex and less unequivocal political reality bears within it the possibility of a religious innovation that has the potential of thrusting radical religious groups into confrontation with the Jewish religious establishment.

Notes

1. G. Herbert, *Fundamentalism and the Church* (Philadelphia, 1957); R. Hofstadter, *Anti-Intellectualism in American Life* (New York, 1963).

2. Neturei Karta ("Guardians of the City," in the religious-spiritualistic sense) emerged against the backdrop of the confrontation between the Zionists and anti-Zionists in Palestine under British mandate during the *yishuv* period (1917–48). See M. Friedman, *Society and Religion: The Non-Zionist Orthodoxy in Eretz-Israel* (Jerusalem, 1978), especially pp. 365–66 [Hebrew]. See also N. Lamm, "The Ideology of Neturei Karta According to the Satmar Version," *Tradition* 13 (1971).

3. Amram Blau died on July 5, 1974; Aharon Katzenelbogen died on December 13, 1978.

4. A community in Jerusalem, which incorporates within it those who do not recognize the State of Israel as a legitimate Jewish political entity. Founded in 1918, the Edah Haredit evolved into an isolationist religious community representing the religious elements that rejected the aspirations of Zionism in Palestine.

5. Agudat Israel initially was organized in 1912 as part of the struggle against the processes of change and secularization undergone by the Jews in Europe since the second half of the eighteenth century. Chiefly represented in this movement were traditional-religious groups that objected to any change in the traditional Jewish way of life. After the establishment of Israel this movement adopted a more moderate political stance, and it now takes part in the country's political life.

6. For an expanded treatment of this subject, see M. Friedman, "Haredi Jewry Confronts the Modern City," in *Studies in Contemporary Jewry*, ed. P. Medding, vol. 2 (Bloomington, Ind., 1985).

7. Numbers 25:1–15.

8. *Babylonian Talmud*, Sanhedrin 81a, 82b.

9. Ibid.

10. *Der Id* (Yiddish weekly of Satmar Hassidim, published in New York City) (May 11, 1984).

11. Many illustrations of this can be found in J. Katz, *Exclusiveness and Tolerance: Jewish-Gentile Relations in Medieval and Modern Times* (London, 1961; New York, 1962).

12. For a detailed treatment of this subject, see M. Friedman, *Society and Religion*, pp. 146–84.

13. Hamizrahi (short for "spiritual counter" in Hebrew), founded by Rabbi Isaac Reines in 1902, expressed the desire of Orthodox circles in Judaism to be integrated into the activity of the Zionist movement and to adapt to the values and ways of life of modern society, while also maintaining a binding affinity to *halakhah*.

14. Rabbi Kook served as the first chief rabbi of Palestine (1921–35). On his philosophical outlook see especially Z. Yaron, *Mishnato shel ha-Rav Kook* (Jerusalem, 1974).

15. For a detailed treatment of this subject, see M. Friedman, "The NRP in Transition: Behind the Party's Decline," in *The Roots of Begin's Success: The 1981 Israeli Election*, ed. D. Caspi et al. (London and New York, 1984), pp. 141–68.

Contributors

Ervand Abrahamian, a professor of history at Baruch College, CUNY, is the author of *Iran between Revolutions* and most recently, *The Iranian Mojahedin.*

Steve Bruce is a professor of sociology at the University of Aberdeen, Scotland. He is the author of several works on Protestantism, including *The Rise and Fall of the New Christian Right; Firm in the Faith: The Survival of Conservative Protestantism; Pray TV: Televangelism in America;* and "Modernity and Fundamentalism: The New Christian Right in America" (*British Journal of Sociology*).

John A. Coleman, S. J., professor of sociology at the Jesuit School of Theology in Berkeley, California, has written *The Evolution of Dutch Catholicism* and *An American Strategic Theology.*

Menachem Friedman is an associate professor of sociology at Bar-Ilan University, Ramat Gan, Israel. He is the author of *Society and Religion: The New Zionist Orthodoxy,* as well as articles dealing with religion and politics in Israel.

Rabbi Arthur Hertzberg is a professor of religion at both Dartmouth College and Columbia University. He has just published a history of Jews in the United States and has written widely on many different aspects of Jewish history, from ancient times to the present.

Lawrence Kaplan, professor of history at the City College of the City University of New York, is the author of *Politics and Religion during the English Revolution.*

Martin E. Marty, a university professor at the University of Chicago, has written approximately 40 books and is senior editor of *Christian Century.* He currently chairs the American Academy of Arts and Sciences's five-year comparative study of world fundamentalism.

Valentine M. Moghadam is a sociologist working for the World Institute for Development Economics Research in Helsinki, Finland. She is the author of several articles dealing with the effects of Islamic fundamentalism on women.

Leo P. Ribuffo, a professor of history at George Washington University, is the author of *The Old Christian Right* and is currently working on a biography of President Jimmy Carter.

Emmanuel Sivan from the Hebrew University of Jerusalem, has taught at Princeton University and has written and edited several works; the best known in this country is *Radical Islam.*

Index

Abortion, 51, 91
Activism
  conservative Protestants and, 33–34, 43–44
  Islamic resurgence and, 103
  Jewish zealots and, 165–68
  potential for, 22
Affirmative action, 41
Afghanistan
  impact of Saur Revolution in, 137–40
  1980s conditions in, 142–44
  patriarchy in, 133–37, 140–42
  political activities of women in, 139–40, 142–43, 144–46
  political struggle in, 126–28
  social structure of, 128–33
Afghan Women's Council (AWC), 141, 142, 144–46, 149
Afshar, Haleh, 129
Agudat Israel (organization), 161, 162, 163, 175 n.5
Alexander, Daniel, 76, 84, 85–86
Alkalai, Yehudah, 153, 154
Ambiguity, 21, 111–14
American Catholicism. *See also* Catholic integralism
  biblical fundamentalism and, 76, 77–80
  Pentecostal movement within, 80–82
American politics. *See also* Politics
  fundamentalist activism in, 33–34
  rightward shift in, 40–42
Amin, Hafizullah, 139, 141
Anti-Communism, 11, 44, 91
Antimodernism, 6, 85–86, 106–7. *See also* Modernity
Anti-Zionist fundamentalists, 170, 173. *See also* Agudat Israel; Edah Haredit; Neturei Karta ("Guardians of the City")
"Armed prophets," 152, 154, 156, 157–58. *See also* Kook, Rabbi Abraham Isaac; Religious Zionism
Ashbrook, John, 47
Ashkenazim, 157, 164, 165
Authoritarian societies, 8–10. *See also* Afghanistan; Muslim countries; *specific nations*
Authority. *See also* Sacred texts
  for Catholic vs. Protestant fundamentalists, 76–77, 84

characteristics of fundamentalism and, 20, 75
  modernity as erosion of, 75–77
  Muslim law (shari'a) as, 106, 107
AWC. *See* Afghan Women's Council (AWC)

Bakker, Jim, 36, 69
Beecher, Henry Ward, 25–26, 27
Bell, Daniel, 24–25, 34–35, 36
Bellah, Robert N., 74
Benigni, Umberto, 77, 86–87
Berger, P. L., 58
Bergstrom, Chuck, 55
Biblical fundamentalism
  within Catholicism, 80–82
  Protestant challenge to Catholics and, 76–80
Biblical higher criticism, 26–27, 82
Binder, Leonard, 98
Blau, Amram, 160, 161–62
Bloch, Marc, 16
Bob Jones University, 47–48, 50
Boesen, Inger, 132, 135
Brideprice, 134, 136
Briggs, Charles, 28
Brown scare, 34
Bryan, William Jennings, 27, 31, 32, 33, 87
Buchanan, John, 55
Bush, George, 68–69

Cannon, Bishop James, 33
Carter, Jimmy, 38, 40
Catholic Answers (organization), 78
Catholic charismatics. *See* Pentecostal movement, in Catholicism
Catholic church. *See* American Catholicism; Catholic integralism
Catholic integralism
  choice of fundamentals in, 19–20
  classical, 82–87
  compared with Protestant fundamentalism, 76, 84–89
  contemporary resurgence of, 89–91
  fascism and, 87
  influence of, 92
  politics and, 91
  as reaction against modernity, 5, 76, 77
Catholic scholasticism, 77